POEMS
OF THE
AZTEC
PEOPLES

Bilingual Press/Editorial Bilingüe

General Editor
Gary D. Keller

Managing Editor
Karen S. Van Hooft

Senior Editor
Mary M. Keller

Editorial Board
Juan Goytisolo
Francisco Jiménez
Eduardo Rivera
Severo Sarduy
Mario Vargas Llosa

Address
Bilingual Press
Department of Foreign Languages
and Bilingual Studies
217 New Alexander
EASTERN MICHIGAN UNIVERSITY
Ypsilanti, Michigan 48197
(313) 487-0042

POEMS
OF THE
AZTEC
PEOPLES

translated and introduced by

EDWARD KISSAM

and

MICHAEL SCHMIDT

Bilingual Press/Editorial Bilingüe

YPSILANTI, MICHIGAN

Cover design by Christopher J. Bidlack

'. . . and the paintings with which they kept their records are gone, because (the conquerors) . . . burnt them in the royal palaces of Nezahualpitzintli, in a great apartment which was the central archive of their papers, where all their ancient heritage was painted; which today their descendants lament with great sorrow, for they remain as in darkness, without record or memory of the deeds of their ancestors.'

JUAN BAUTISTA POMAR
Relación de Tezcoco
(*Mexico, ed. Icazbalceta*, 1891)

Acknowledgments

Versions by Michael Schmidt first appeared in
*Antaeus, Carcanet, Journals of Pierre Menard,
New Measure* and *The Island*; versions by Edward
Kissam in *Alcheringa, Anonym, Antaeus, Bricoleur,
A Curriculum of the Soul* (fasc. 13), *Prairie
Schooner, Shaking the Pumpkin* (ed. Jerome
Rothenberg, Doubleday, 1972) and
The Sham Flyers by Edward Kissam (Anvil, 1969).

I should like to thank Dr Kasia Wionczeck,
Dr J. L. Díaz G. and Alfred Bush who supplied me
with texts that were otherwise unavailable. — E.K.

Contents

Note on Pronunciation

As a rough guide, Aztec names are pronounced as though written in Spanish, with the following exceptions:

ll is a double *l* as in 'soul love'
x is pronounced much as *sh* in Engli*sh*
c is pronounced as English *k*
h in *hu* and *ha* is pronounced as English *w*
terminal *h* is pronounced as the *h* in English '*h*ow'
n nasalizes the preceding vowel as in French 'on'
i is rather closer to English *ee* as in 'feet' than to *i* in Spanish

Generally, primary stress falls on the first syllable of a word, and in compound words a secondary stress is evident in the first syllable of the second word, e.g. *N*ezahual*c*oyotl.

Introduction

Smoke rises, the mist
is spreading.

Weep, my friends,
and know that by these deeds
we have forever lost our heritage.

THIS VALEDICTION concludes one of the last Aztec poems, composed when the Spaniards were beginning their wholesale suppression of native culture in Mexico in 1521. The poem laments the fall of the great island capital of the Aztecs, Tenochtitlan, the warriors' flight across the lake, and their premonition of a total loss of heritage in the face of the brutal, mysterious conquerors. The Aztec empire, already under strain before Cortez arrived, was simply snuffed out — and worse, the palaces and temples, the schools and ceremonial centres, with all that they contained of artefacts and archives, were pillaged, burnt out, or razed systematically. The Indians blamed their own cowardice for their defeat — but more than cowardice was involved. The strange men with guns and horses seemed to have stepped out of vital legend: native astrologers had long predicted some such advent. The Aztec empire was in decay, and even had Spain not come, Tenochtitlan, with its warring sun-cult of Huitzilopochtli-Tonatiuh and its expansionist dreams, was vulnerable to its own flaws — its military and administrative over-extension, its unpopularity, its institutional weaknesses. Nonetheless, the traumatic sudden loss of all that they had built and made, and the consequent relentless suppression of all that they had thought and discovered, amounted to the extermination of a rich and complex culture, not merely another modification of the Indian power structure. Previously tribe had built on tribe, culture on culture, and each had learned from its predecessors the lessons of science, art and institution. This was the end of a long evolutionary process towards a sophisticated native society with its roots in a rich tradition. One of the last poets laments:

In grief we beat our fists
against the walls of our mud houses,
a net of holes our only heritage.

In their origins, the Aztecs were a barbaric nomad tribe from northern Mexico. Their rapid ascent to power in less than a century, and the opulence of the great capital of their empire, gave them a sense of being elect among the tribes, of ethnic superiority to their vassals. They were the chosen of the Sun. Their function was to keep the sun in circuit. Their world was the fifth creation, theirs the fifth Sun. The previous creations had each been destroyed by elemental forces. This fifth was equally vulnerable – a precarious balance, a delicate tension between the four elements and the four cardinal directions. The myth of the five creations was inherited from previous cultures. The Aztecs, however, saw themselves as actively involved in the play of elements, maintaining the fifth sun: it had to be sustained and nourished with human strength – by the 'flowered war' which led to the recruitment of sacrificial victims, whether for the gift to the sun of living hearts, or for the transmission of human energy to the Sun by flaying sacrificial victims, where the priest donned the skin of the flayed man and danced to Huitzilopochtli-Tonatiuh, the god of war, the sun. This was the ceremony of Xippe Totec.

This grotesque ceremonial, the Aztecs' addition to an inherited mythology and structure of rituals, was dictated as much by political necessity as by religious zeal. Conquest meant that thousands of prisoners were brought back from the wars to the capital. The state could ill tolerate the threat of so large a body of alien, hostile men in the heart of its capital, while its armies were off annexing more territory or pacifying tribes already annexed. Furthermore, it was an irritating expense to feed and house prisoners. Better to be rid of them – and how better to justify their disposal, and to justify the wars, than to call each action holy, to harness religion in the service of imperial ambitions? The Sun's elected tribe found it easy to accept this extension of the myth, referring all their military action to the sun cult, reducing war and sacrifice to grand and potent ritual.

A number of the poems in this anthology relate to the war cult, to the two orders of knights – 'tiger warriors' (more properly called 'ocelot warriors') and 'eagle warriors' – who are celebrated allusively. Poems with eagle and tiger imagery usually refer to the warriors in their symbolic involvement – the knights wore uniforms made of ocelot skins or plumes, with elaborate headgear. Other military references, tribal and symbolic, are explained in the Glossary. Not all the war poems celebrate the battle or the faith – some lament the loss of kin and friend, the deceit of allies, the impersonality and apparent insignificance of the sacrifice. But the dominant strains are those of celebration and the symbolic recapitulation of specific campaigns.

Poetically, more important than the celebrations of war are the lyrical, philosophical and mythological poems. These were composed by the princes and priests. The mythology of the poems derives in part from Toltec tradition – especially the references to the myth of Quetzalcoatl, the 'plumed serpent'. The Aztec authorities had done their utmost to transmute the traditions of their sophisticated ancestors – but they had not succeeded. The Toltec culture was highly civilized and humane. Its rise had been almost as spectacularly sudden as that of the Aztecs. Its decline is cloaked in mystery. It left a tradition of crafts, of architecture and astronomy, legend and myth, to the many tribes with which it had come in contact in central and southern Mexico. The Toltec lesson was not easily forgotten – the tribe itself became a haunting legend. To the mind of Aztec and vassal princes who felt dissatisfied or disgusted with the war cult, Toltec tradition represented an alternative, a humane vision.

Quetzalcoatl, the 'plumed serpent' or the 'plumed twin', had been identified with one of the kings of the Toltecs – the blond god, the pale king who had taught them all they knew of heaven and earth, who as a god had, with considerable self-sacrifice, redeemed the bones of man from the underworld and remade him under the fifth Sun (poem 58). The poetry abounds with explicit and implicit allusions to him. Through him, the Toltec contribution to the Aztec poetry of 'dissent' was immeasurable. The consuming sense of the ephemerality of earthly life and pleasure, the increasing tendency to monotheism with stress on 'Ometeotl-Omecihuatl', the gods of duality, and Ipalnemoani, 'the one for whom all things live', in the late poems, as well as the basic humanity and the almost decadent melancholy of this alternative tradition, can be traced back in origin largely to Toltec and related legend, though what was made of the legend was highly original. And other tribal legends and cults – for instance, the fertility cults – contributed to the rich culture which subverted, in conscience at least, the war cult.

Philosophically obsessed with ephemerality, depressed by the growing responsibilities of a faltering empire, and astrologically forewarned of the advent of strange visitors from another world – creatures that would emerge from legend and bring unknown visitations on the Aztec people – it can well be imagined that the Aztecs were almost anticipating the Spaniards, that they were prepared for submission. Of course, they fought. But their vassals turned on them, their king Moctezuma proved cowardly, his successor died of smallpox, their last king was tortured and executed. Then began the rigorous suppression of their culture, a suppression on the surface remarkably successful, though pockets of the old ideologies survived long after the Conquest, and vestiges of them still remain, especially in the southern and western regions of Mexico.

Fortunately, a number of the early friars took more than a missionary interest in the people they had come to convert. Some of them learned the native languages, some proved skilful early ethnographers and took down from dictation versions of the old songs, legends and myths. Fray Bernadino de Sahagún must rate as the first and finest chronicler, taking down book after book of information: poems from the oral tradition, historical testimony, catalogues of customs and rituals, and recorded impressions. This is how the poems in this anthology survived – in large manuscript volumes now published, with translations into Spanish and extensive annotations, by Angel María Garibay especially, and Miguel León-Portilla, among others. Partially, the chronicling seems to have been prompted almost by a sense of charity. Juan Bautista Pomar, one of the chroniclers, recalls in his *Relación de Tezcoco* (Mexico, 1582) the effect the cultural extermination had on the native people.

... and the paintings with which they kept their records are gone, because [the conquerors and clerics] burnt them in the royal palaces of Nezahualpitzintli, in a great apartment which was the central archive of their papers, where all their ancient heritage was painted; which today their descendants mourn, for they remain as in darkness, without record or memory of the deeds of their ancestors.

The primary motive behind the chroniclers, however, was curiosity, and perhaps a sense that, with a clearer understanding of the minds of the people to whom they were preaching, they might better serve the purposes of conversion and education in the Roman Catholic tradition. Sahagún records that:

It is well known that the caves, forests and thickets where today the damned adversary [the Devil] hides are the chants and psalms they have composed and sing to him, without understanding what is in them.

But Sahagún was himself so in sympathy with his native informants that on two occasions his papers were confiscated. The Spanish authorities feared his work might prove subversive back in Spain, where it was popularly believed that the Conquest had brought peace, culture and religion to a totally barbarous land.

Yet even Sahagún found his material at times obscure and unintelligible and, probably, evil in its obscurity. Only recently have we come to recognize the barriers to our understanding of non-European or 'primitive' cultures. As Claude Lévi-Strauss points out in *The Savage Mind*, 'primitive' cultures are not incapable of logical thought – they don't need it. Their world vision is not confused but fused: its habit is to see things whole, to observe the universal in the particular. This vision is different from ours, not inferior to it. But this is the main barrier which divides us from a culture not only unfamiliar but alien – a mode of thought which does not analyse and particularize but synthesizes areas and levels of experience which we would not naturally relate – except in poetry. For this reason, perhaps, our most fruitful access to Aztec thought and culture is through the poetry.

The poems we have translated are from a number of sources. *Cantares Mexicanos*, which is the source of much of the remaining poetry, includes poems from Tenochtitlan, as well as poems from Chalco, Huexotzinco, and Texcoco, city states with subtly different cultures and dialects from the Aztec. It would be more correct for us to speak of Nahuatl rather than Aztec poetry, since many of the finest poems come from cultures related to the Aztecs linguistically, but peripheral to the Tenochtitlan tradition, part of it only as tributary states are a part, culturally, of the chief state in an empire. Besides the Tenochtitlan tradition, there are two other major traditions: that of Tlaxcala and that of the Otomí nation. Even the

Aztec scribe working with Olmos and Sahagún in compiling the *Cantares Mexicanos* records that the Otomí poems were unintelligible and alien to him.

The problem of obscurity in the poems is not entirely a matter of ignorance on our part. We would be grateful for more information, but obscurity is often more a matter of the Indian poet's attitude than of our scanty information. The pervasive attitude of any nation which has made major advances of its own is one of pride: the poets of that nation take for granted certain beliefs and prejudices to which we have no access. This attitude raises other barriers between the poems and our understanding of them, if we feel that understanding includes finding them interesting as something more than mere antiquities.

In reading the poems we do not need to know the cultural tensions that gave rise to them, the rivalries of the fertility, war, and Toltec mythologies. More important to bear in mind is the fact that the poems were aristocratic. We know of no poet who was not a noble. The Aztec princes and their vassal princes were poets as a matter of course. In an oral tradition, this helps to account for the similarity of styles and the lack of personal idiosyncrasies. It also accounts – oral poetry by definition conserves traditional elements – for the subversive 'Toltec' content of some of the princes' greatest poems – justifiable enough in the case of the puppet kings, who might well feel dissatisfaction with the war cult. We can't but wonder, however, if the great war lords, the wielders of empire, realized what they were at times saying about the fruitlessness of their activity. Perhaps, within the limits of convention, they did, and considered their utterances a ceremonial duty rather than a vital mode of expression. Or perhaps what they believed as princes and generals involved in 'flowered war' for the Sun did not fully satisfy them as individual men in specific human situations.

The Spanish conquest introduced into Mexico an advanced technology, and by removing most of the motives for native initiative, ironically reinforced – especially in the southern parts of Mexico – the old 'pagan' system of thought which hundreds of missionaries had come to New Spain to stamp out. In the outlying regions, attempts to teach the natives Spanish were in most cases half-hearted. Nahuatl and, in the south,

Mayan dialects were spoken for many generations, and are still in use, as are dialects of Zapotec, Otomí, and many others. This ecclesiastical negligence permitted cultural isolation and the transmission of a distinctly native religion under a veneer of Christianity. Modern anthropologists have unearthed this archaic tradition among the more accessible tribes in Mexico and Central America, and some of this material is translated in the Appendix.

It is interesting in the contemporary Indian poems to note that, when the Conquest destroyed a native system of thought which had managed to relate religion and ritual to every aspect of social life, the natives returned to the oldest form of religious experience and expression known: individual revelation through ecstasy. This is manifested in the practice of shamanism and magic, closely associated with the religious use of psychedelic substances. The concept of the *nahual*, the spirit-soul, prevalent among North American Indian tribes, was at the time of the Conquest a minor feature of Aztec religion. Magic was accepted as a fact, but not accorded major importance. Before the Conquest the idea of individual revelation had been lost, as well as the practice of medicine by a shaman to combat soul-loss or to remove magical objects from the body. But the later cultures, in their relative isolation, have evolved a religion and an oral literature deriving much from the individual revelation of the shaman in his ecstatic state, ceremonially induced by the eating of psychedelic substances. Though none of the recent poems compares technically or in depth of thought with the earlier Indian poems, they have the rhythmical and symbolic quality of the earlier lyrical poems, altered and darkened by the mysterious revived ceremonial.

In an oral poetic tradition like the Aztec, technique and form are especially complex and exacting – strong rhythm, alliteration, epithets, repetition of syntactical structures and refrains being essential mnemonic devices. Aztec poetry is as complex as Celtic oral poetry, and shares many of the devices of that tradition.

The Aztec language is synthetic rather than analytic: it builds up phrases conjugated from word units and particles. Each phrase is composed of several fused elements. In a real sense, it is misleading to speak of 'words' in an oral poetic tradition. The poets spoke or sang units of meaning – bundles of sound assembled into one long phrase in which the word units were so fused as to be merely tributary elements to a single, precise symbol or meaning. Each of these complex phrases was rhythmically constructed and related to other phrases in its context rhythmically, alliteratively, and semantically. This quality is, of course, impossible to bring out in translation. We have tried in our lineation to reflect to some degree the phrasing effect of individual lines.

Not only is the language synthetic. So, as we mentioned above, is the vision and the process of thought – or, more precisely, intuition – behind the poems. The poems have a severely restricted vocabulary, consisting mainly of flower, stone, bird, animal, war and scent imagery. Not only mnemonics prompt this limitation. Each poem relates to various levels of thought: literal, philosophical, mythical, and religious. The poetry tries to integrate these levels in a single statement, and only a small number of symbolic terms is common to all levels. The process resembles that of consistent medieval allegory, though allegory is a conscious attempt at integration, while the Aztec poems come from a tradition of fused vision and are not didactic but almost magical or visionary in the complex transcendence of their thought.

Take the word unit *xóchitl*, for example. Literally this means 'flower'. In a special Aztec construction, where two images release an abstract meaning, *in xóchitl in cuícatl* ('flower and song') means 'poetry', just as 'beauty' is sometimes rendered 'jade and lush feathers', and 'divine transcendency' becomes 'night and tempest'. *Xóchitl*, on its first symbolic level, means 'word' – the word spoken by the wise man or the singer, who is often shown in the murals and codices as emitting flowers from his mouth in complicated ascending scrolls. With reference to the solar cult, *xóchitl* comes to symbolize the heart given in sacrifice, or the warrior's heart or body given in battle, or simply blood, the body's flower. With regard to myth, it symbolizes the gift of life, the flower from the Tree of Life, and perhaps the individual *nahual* or spirit-soul. Finally, in its philosophical sense, it is the prime symbol for ephemerality. Most of the words used in the poetry have a similar transcendence of meaning – we mentioned above, for example, the images of 'eagle' and 'tiger'. In the phrases that make up the poem, each element is charged with an almost ideogrammatic complexity of meaning and must always be seen as intersecting various planes of thought. 'The body makes a few flowers/then falls away withered somewhere', one of the poems says. This can be seen as referring to the ephemerality of life, to self-sacrifice, to the creation of poems, to the generation of children.

Originality in Aztec poetry was a matter of variation on strict traditional themes, not innovation. Generally the poems are structured in stanzas, either contrasting or dialectically contradicting one another, giving the effect of internal dialogue. Or they assemble a complex of images to embody a matrix of ideas. Sahagún typified the native artists as men who 'communicate with their own hearts'.

The native metres have not been adequately explored. In translation, we have not tried to reproduce them, as they seem essentially alien to English stress patterns. The simplest metres are four-stress, usually with eight or ten syllables and generally consistent. The more meditative poems are composed in longer rhythmical phrases, of twelve to fourteen syllables, with four or six stresses. Usually the line ends with a rhythmic phrase which does not contribute to the meaning (*Ohuaya, Yeehuaya, Aya*) but was probably chanted by the chorus as a refrain. Refrains are often more subtle, a phrase repeated in slightly divergent forms to give the effect of phrasal punning and to produce rhythmic unity, assonance, and rhyme. Music and dance played a large part in recitation, and we should bear this in mind while reading what are, in a sense, scores for a far more elaborate art form than simply a verbal one. We have inherited only one part of the complex ritual.

As translators, we are not linguists. We have only a limited knowledge of Nahuatl, and our translations depend largely on Garibay's and León-Portilla's Spanish versions and excellent annotations of the poems. We have selected the more translatable poems and fragments, and excluded those whose obscurity makes them reluctant to cross over into English. We have provided in the Glossary explanations of the more difficult allusions.

We have tried to be true to the text and to the reader, resolving some complexities without, we hope, falsifying the tone of the poems. Undoubtedly many of the elements central to the Aztec poems have evaded our translation – but our technique in translating does, we hope, carry some of the lucidity and vitality of the originals. We have tried where possible to return to the source in human experience of the poetry. If we have been able to recreate the stance, the movement of the poems, something of them may still endure, relevant to the modern reader as once to a sophisticated audience more fully involved in the ceremony of song than any audience before or since.

EDWARD KISSAM *and* MICHAEL SCHMIDT

1

Songs of Life

1

Shake the flower,
root out song
in your house, Ipalnemoani,
Master of Herons.
     —Rejoice!

Perhaps with words
you will be pierced, broken
to understand,
Prince Warriors:
       earth is all over with.
     —Rejoice!

2

Only he, Ipalnemoani . . .
I did not know . . .
Never know him? Never know?
I was joyless among men.

You rained down joy,
your wealth and wisdom,
mercifully, Ipalnemoani,
fragrant priceless flowers.

I longed for them.
I did not know.

3

Blue birds, black birds, come
where the tree of blossoms grows —
its precious clustered leaves!
Come dark birds, blue birds,
and you, green quetzal!
    You come from Nonohualco,
the land by the water,
precious birds of Ipalnemoani.
You are his creatures. Come!

Here, in the house of moss,
spread like a flower
is the head-dress of the blue bird.
He came to contemplate the dawn.
    All your birds are waking.
The gold tzinitzcan preens,
the red quechol, the blue bird
who screams the dawn.
    Their morning
wakens you.

4

Ipalnemoani,
do you live
inside the sky?

For you hold this city
in your arms,
the land between the waters
rests on your palm.

Everywhere men pray
for you to be strong.
But you live
inside the sky
and hold this city
in your arms,
the land between the waters
rests on your palm.

5   Place of Making

The flower of Tamoanchan is sweet.
I offer the red flower in Tamoanchan.
      It is your heart's book,
      your song, Ipalnemoani.
You know its meaning
and its offering.
Each man finds in it his colour
and rejoices.

Your heart: your song.

Our despair is woven to a precious thing:
your song, Ipalnemoani.

6 The Tree of Life

Blossomed tree stands up in Tamoanchan
we were created there, we came to be there
there, the thread of our lives was strung
by the force which all things live for.

That is how I work gold,
how I polish jade,

it is the grace of my song.

It is as though it were turquoise.

It spun us around
four times
there in Tamoanchan
for which all things live.

7 Dialogue

    i I am come
      from the ocean
      waves
      where water is dyed
      with the morning.

   ii (I am just
      a singer.

My heart
is a flower!
I offer—my song.)

i I am from the rainland,
come to please the deity!

ii (I am just
a singer.
My heart
is a flower!
I offer—my song.)

8

Ipalnemoani,
you tint all things
with flowers,
sing them full
of colour,
whatever lives on earth.
The ties of war are broken:
only as you paint us
do we live on earth.

. . .

in the palace
still
in a jade chest
concealed
the princes can be found:
like them
we too are mortal . . .

9   Love Song of Warriors

They say
I am come to guard the mountain.
Ipalnemoani
paints the poet's heart
with flowers. In your palace,
Prince Tlaltecatzin,
you are alone, you sigh, lament,
you are fused with my god,
Ipalnemoani.

He is proud, your garland
draws his passion, you, the red macaw,
lovely woman, sweet mother, flower.
You lend yourself to others.
    But you will be abandoned.
    All of us
    will wither from our bodies.

Beauty!
You have come before lords,
open to love on my mat of feathers —
blue-jay, yellow parrot, quetzal feathers.
You stand there
precious, scented blossom.
You lend yourself to others.
    But you will be abandoned.
    All of us
    will wither from our bodies.

The flowering chocolate
catches fire.

We share out
the tobacco flower.
If I do not taste with my heart
I will grow drunk.

. . .

I alone am sad,
   'Why must I leave
   for the place where the bodiless dwell?
   I am a poet!
   My flowers are gold.'

I leave
and look back towards my house:
the rows of flowers . . .

. . .

Huge emeralds,
the broad fan
of quetzal plumes —
will these buy off death?

One day I leave,
go losing
myself.

Lord, I surrender!
I cry,
'Let me, the poet,
be shrouded, be gone!
Who can overcome
that destiny?'

Alone,
my heart under flowers,
I shall go.
Fine plumes are torn,
the emeralds, all precious,
will be splinters.

Let it be
to peace.

10

Here
    let our songs, our flowers
    be three
to lull our hatred,
to lull our sadness.

Friends
    rejoice: we live
    on earth briefly.
Only friendship
should fill us!

11

emeralds and
flowers fall
     like rain —

your song!
as you are
singing

in Mexico

the sun is shining!

(*Motecuhzoma II*)

12

The butterfly
sipping:
the flower
my open heart,
friends,
a fragrant flower.

Now I scatter it
as rain.

13 Butterfly

What
are you thinking,
thinking,
friend?
Do you like songs?
Are you after
the flowers of God?
Rejoice among the drums!
. . . or go away, as you please.

The petal butterfly
flutters, flutters
                and tastes
the honey of our flowers.
He weaves among our sprays,
our fans and flutes, rejoicing
in our drums.
    Rejoice!

14

And what
does that sacred bird sing
where the ililin grows?

. . .

open-winged
the butterfly
wanders the flowers

to drink,
rejoice,

its open heart!
its heart a flower!

15

Flowers have come!
  to refresh
  and delight you, princes.
You see them briefly
as they dress themselves,
spread their petals,
perfect only in spring —
countless golden flowers!

The flowers have come
to the skirt of the mountain!

16

Yellow flowers,
sweet flowers,

precious vanilla flowers
the crow's dark magic flowers

weave themselves together.

They are your
flowers, god.

We only borrow them:
your flowered drum,
your bells,
your song:

they are your flowers,
god.

17

The flowers are budding,
are now beautiful
inside, in the golden hut
of the white Otomi

You were proud of your ear-rings
    of red obsidian,

you Mexicans,
there in the golden hut
of the white Otomí.

18

A beautiful pheasant sings
over the flowers
and his songs unleash
the lord of the world.

Only his own kind answer him.

Your heart is a book of paintings, singer,
you came to sing and sound your drum.

It's simply that in spring
you make men happy.

(*Nezahualcoyotl*)

19 Song to the God of Nets and Oars

You live by the lake, you
who nourish.

It is difficult
to feed the god.
Opochtli is my god
I must
feed him carefully
like a precious bird,

who rules
the water
it is difficult

I feed him
like a precious bird.

20

I've come this far,
to the boughs of the flowering tree.
I'm the flowered hummingbird:
I please my nose and feel happy.
My lips taste sweet and good.

21 Bird and Drum Song

Rejoice, my friends: I thump the drum
and sing totototo
       tiquiti
       tiquiti!

Let the graceful flowers sing
in Totoquihuatzin's house
       totiquiti
       toti
       totototo
       tiquiti
       tiquiti!

My heart is jewels
       totototo
my robe of flowers is gold,
the flowers that I'll give one day
in praise!
       totiquiti
       toti
       totototo
       tiquiti
       tiquiti!

Ho! Sing the song in your heart!
       totototo
take these wreaths of roses, painted books
       totiquiti
       toti
which I will give one day
in homage!
       totiquiti
       totiquiti
       tiquiti
       tiquiti!

I come
to the patio of flowers:
my word a song
my thought a flower.
   My drumbeat
   is an open book.

I praise
    the one
      who is adored
      in every place,
    I beg his pity.
War lords, am I right
to seek him?
I, Moctezuma, am uncertain.

        Moctezuma, painter of books,
        you come
        to the patio of flowers
        to sing.
        Blue-green bird,
        you sway on your perch
        before god.
           Yellow butterfly,
        you alight!

           Moctezuma cools us
        with fans of flowers
        where we lie
        on these carpets
        woven out of leaves.

23

I come
to weave you in my chains of feathers.
I spread divans of tzinitzcan feathers,
crown you with the feathers of the bright macaw.
Brightness robes you.
In trembling green quetzal feathers
I bind you to each other,
my gathered friends!

Our love grows stronger, singing.
I carry friendship to the palaces
where we can lie content until
we journey to the dead.
Then we will have loaned
love to one another.

I come
to plant my songs,
make them grow for you.
God sent me, I possess his flowers:
my duty to weave love chains on the earth.

(*Temilotzin*)

24

What were you thinking?
    Where was your heart wandering?

as you pour out your heart
as you do not hold it to a fixed direction,
you will destroy your heart,
yourself.

Are you going to extinguish yourself on earth?

Come back,
    hear the lovely song:
refresh your heart with the nectar of flowers.
They are fragrant
where my song lifts up,

I who sing to delight Ipalnemoani,
Lord of what is near and with you

. . .

Leave the cloudy shadow,
come back with us:
raise a new song,
    as I who sing

raise up my song
to please the Lord of All Things,

if someone appears in the dwelling of your heart.

25   Tenochtitlan

The city is spread out.
It spirals in circles of green jade,
radiating splendid light,
such plumes of paradise quetzal
are Mexico.

At the edge of the city
the boats leave and return:
the warriors.

A flowered cloud covers the people.
It is your house here,
Ipalnemoani, you rule here
and care for us.

Your song is heard in Anahuac.
It spreads over the people.
Palace of white willows,
palace of white reeds
is Mexico.

And you, as a blue heron,
spread your wings over the city,
you fly to the city. You spread
your tail and wings.
Your servants rule it all.

. . .

Let there be no pleasure
in wandering
lost in sadness.

Who will serve Ipalnemoani,
who sustains heaven and earth?
His command blazes
like a bonfire.
In all four corners
dawn fires the warrior's voice.

This is the city of Motecuzoma
and of Acolhuacan, of Nezahualpilli.
The throng leaves with fans of quetzal plumes,
they leave in boats, full of sighs,
full of sadness:

What will become of the city of Tenochtitlan?
What will the god decide?

26

In Spring, the flowers spring up,
spread their petals
in the face of Life given out.
You have an answer —
the precious spirit hummingbird
you searched for.
How many have gained
from your songs! You gave them heart.
The flowers
are moving in the wind.

(*Monencuauhtzin*)

27

Where will I go, where will I go?
Two things spring up hard, hard:
    There to your dwelling
        down
    or to the inside sky
        or here
        down
    upon the earth?

28

Your lovely song
rises like a whirring hawk.
You raise it beautifully.
You are surrounded by flowers.
You sing in the flowered branches.

Are you from Ipalnemoani?
Has your god spoken to you?

You saw the dawn
and set yourself to song.

(*Ayocuan*)

29

In Spring the golden corn in bloom
sets us in motion,
the cream-coloured tender ear
becomes our light;
and to know our friends' hearts
are faithful
leaves a jewel necklace
hung around our necks.

(*Ayocuan*)

30

Suffering roots in me, my song is nothing.
I'm only a squirrel skittering through the hills.
My friends are happy: maybe they're precious jade
maybe their hearts are like books, painted
with careful wisdom.
                    I want them . . .

oh their song has stopped,
those who are coming from where the yucca blooms,

perhaps they are jade
perhaps their hearts are a painting.

31

I have only come to sing.
What do you say, friends?
What are you talking about here?
Here there are flowers.
The dancers, princes
come here crying out
in the middle of spring.
Unequal flowers,
slave and master's song.
In my house, all is suffering.

(*Motenehuatzin*)

32

White dawn, Ipalnemoani,
are we really here, talking . . .
If I were to offer you
jade green as leaves,
give you rich salves,

                  perhaps
if we invoked you
with fineries, ornaments,
the strength of fierce eagles
and fiery tigers . . .

what if no one on earth
is upright
in truth . . .

33 Love Songs

I am scattering
different kinds of flowers.

Here I come to give you songs
to make your head spin, flowers,
as I smile at you.

I come from where the water
gushes out of the earth.
I've come to offer you songs,

flowers to make your head spin.
Oh, another kind of flower
and you know it in your heart.

I came to bring them to you,
I carry them to your house
on my back,

uprooted flowers,
I'm bent double with the weight of them
for you.

Let's go to your house, let's.

Fragrant flowers,
I bring them where you live
where the flowers open.

I offer you pleasure,
flowers I tended, flowers
carefully planted.

The fields flower for our mother.
She bathes in the sun, her feathers
open and spread.

In the house of shining books
the fields are flowering.

34

I come,
I come once more
and sing —

Listen to the song
I scatter.

My songs are known,
their fame grows
and grows,

I am flying, I'll fly
as far as Panotla.

I'm beginning,
now I can sing,
I'm from the heart of Tula,

my voice
breaks over you,
flowers open.

Listen,
listen carefully to my song.

I'm a thief of songs.

How can you
make them yours,

heart?

if you suffer,

treat it as a picture,
trace the lines,
the red and the black,

do it carefully,
draw it well

and perhaps
when they are yours

you will no longer suffer.

35

Only
for sleep we come,
for dreams.

Lie! It is a lie
we come to live on earth.

As a weed we become
each springtime,

swell green, our hearts
open,

the body makes a few flowers
and drops away withered somewhere.

36

I remember —
I came to earth
to perish from the earth.
I am Moquihuix.
Will we live

to see joy perishing?
   I wander,
everywhere I call.
   My heart lives
where the flowers,
where the songs
are spiralling.
Will we see them
perishing?

(*Moquihuix*)

37

I, who cry and suffer,
am out of my head.
Yes, I have this time, the present,
but I remember, and say

If I never died, if I were never to vanish . . .

I should go where there is no death,
where we could win some victory.

If I never died, if I never were to vanish . . .

(probably *Nezahualcoyotl*)

38

Rejoice, rejoice
my flower king:
you own many jewels —

we do not come
again:
only once
your heart knows the earth.

39

Our house on earth
we do not inhabit

only borrow it
briefly
            (be splendid, princes!)

here only
our heart sings
briefly, briefly
lent to one another

earth is not our last home:
take these flowers
            (be splendid, princes!)

40

Interwoven,
    blue and fiery flowers
your heart and word,
    prince Ayocuan.
For one instant
    make them yours
here on earth.

I cry
    because death destroys them
yes,
    destroys what we have done,
those fragile songs.

For an instant
    with the earth
make them yours.

(*Tecayehuatzin*)

41 Cacamatzin's Lament

I, Cacamatzin, speak
only to remember our king,
Nezahualpilli.
Does he converse
with his father king
somewhere among drums?
I remember him.

Who will not go there?
Will the man treasured as gold,
as jewels are treasured,
not go there?
Am I a shield of turquoise tiles,
will they replace the tiles that fall?
Will I become again?
be wound in fine cloth?
On earth, beside these drums,
I commemorate the kings!

(*Cacamatzin*)

42

Will Cacamatl
the eagle prince
return
or Ayocuan
whose arrow pierced the sky?
  Will he delight us again?
Not again — forever gone.

I weep for king Ayocuan,
our strongest lord.
But he has been exalted,
gone among his comrades.

  My father, my mother,
  did they know him
  on earth?

  I weep:
all are in the land
where bodies do not dwell.

43

Could it be true we live on earth?
On earth forever?

Just one brief instant here.

Even the finest stones begin to split,
even gold is tarnished,
even precious bird-plumes
shrivel like a cough.

Just one brief instant here.

(*Nezahualcoyotl*)

44

What am I to go with?
those flowers
which have closed?

Will my name be nothing some time?
Will I leave no thing behind me in the world?

At least flowers, at least songs!
How is my heart to work?

Perhaps we come, in vain, to live,
to come like springs upon dry earth.

(*Ayocuan*)

45

Don't our friends know it?
Heart hurts, is indignant
no second birth
no second time to be a son,
only once do I live in this world.

(*Tlapaltecuautzin*)

46 Cuacuauhtzin's Sad Song

[Nezahualpilli, the poet-king, was Prince Cuacuautzin's over-
lord. One day he fell in love with a girl Cuacuautzin was
raising to be his wife. Nezahualpilli sent his vassal to war to
dispose of him and possess the girl. Before he departed,
Cuacuautzin recited this poem at his farewell feast, lamenting
the painful ephemerality of friendship.]

My heart
longs for flowers.
To hold them!
My song
hurts me.
I, Cuacuautzin,
long for flowers.
But I am forsaken.

Where can we flee
and not be forced to die?
If I were precious stone,
or gold, even gold,
I would be forged,
flattened on the anvil.
Only my life is my own,
forsaken.

Yoyontzin, prince,
you sound your jade drum,
your red and blue conch.
The singer stands to recite to you.
Bring sad hearts for him to relieve,
show him your sad faces here.

Let your heart spread its blossom,
let it wander the sky.
But you hate me,
forsake me to death.
I am bound to Ipalnemoani's palace,
to perish.
Perhaps you will weep for me?

You will wound your heart,
my friend. I leave
for Ipalnemoani's palace.
My heart speaks this farewell,
    'I shall not return,
        nor sprout again on earth.'
I leave you.

My labour — vain.
Friends, rejoice a while.
Will you take no pleasure
from life, my friends?

I shall carry
your beautiful flowers, your songs
with me. I never sang in Spring,
but only now as I am sad,
forsaken, I, Cuacuautzin.
I shall take
your beautiful flowers, your songs
with me.

(*Cuacuautzin*)

2

Ritual Songs

47 Song to Tlaltecuhtli, the Mother of the Gods

Oh! Golden flower opens
spreads its petals, holy thighs,
her face the dark place
we were born from.
She is our mother, she's back
from where all things were born.

Oh your golden flowers!

Oh! Moist white flower opens
spreads its petals, holy thighs,
her face the dark place
we were born from.
She is our mother, she's back
from where all things were born.

She is
there on the cactus, our mother,
the dark obsidian
butterfly that gave us birth.

We saw her there
as we wandered across the endless plains,
there where she fed herself
with the hearts of deer.

She is
our mother whose body is the earth.

She is our mother,
dressed in plumes, painted white
for the sacrifice whose body will be
the earth.

Oh! In all four directions
wherever the winds blow,
the people shoot arrows in search of the gods.

Oh you became a deer in that barren land!
where those two men, Xiuhnel and Mimich,
first saw you.

48   Song of Huitzilopochtli

He was born on a smoking shield,
he is war,
the sun has become a warrior,
he was born
out of the belly of earth.

He was born on a smoking shield,
he is war,
the sun has become a warrior,
he was born
out of the belly of earth.

He is the first,
he leads the way, on Snake Mountain.
His mask
is a shield, the sun rays splaying
in all
four directions, all
over the world.
At the ridge he puts it on.

He is most manly of them all,
most potent.
As he shows himself, as he appears
the earth shakes and trembles,
letting loose

war
they cower before him.

Who
will wear the shield of the sun's rays?
the world
the mask to cover his face.

49   Song of the Mimixcoa

I came from the Seven Caves,
the first place, where magic ruled.
My footprints lead from there,
where the tribes began.

I am born. I am already born.
I was born with my cactus arrows
from the cactus which makes you drunk.

I am born. I came down as song
with my net snare ready.
I was born with my snare.
I was born with my net.

I hold it in one hand, in one
hand I hold it, with my hand.
Oh, with its hand
it will snare.

50 Song of Xochiquetzal

'Have I, Xochiquetzal, plumed lady of flowers,
yet left that greatest place
ruled by mist and rain?'

'Not yet.
I find myself still where I live by the river
in Tamoanchan, in the realm of spirits.'

Lord of the wind,
you have been crying,
young sun,
you search for her,
in the realm of clouds,
of turquoise, blue-green mist —

on our behalf.

51 Midwife's Song to Ayopechtli

In her house of clouds
in cloud banners, liquid necklaces
in water, mist, somewhere

somewhere life
in ripe wombs

Up! Come up!
Let yourself
be sent,
come out,
come,

child, feather
sub-
feathery marine
being.

Come up, come

up, come,
be born, jewel child
come up
come

Here!

Eagle, feathered mother,
circlets of blood
like jewels on her face,

feathered wounded earth
is dressed in green

spring sweeps the earth,
she rules those who sow

she is the cypress, spreading
over them, feathered wings

in our land, ears of corn
rustle, hanging on poles of bells.

Fire-hardened stick in my hand
I pierce the earth. Fire-hardened
stick in my hand

ear of corn planted in holy earth
rustles on a pole of bells.

Feathers, feathers fill my hand
ear of corn floats among bells
rustling, feathered wings.

Eagle, feathered mother
rules us, rules the roots

in earth
sprouting into leaves.

The blossom, agave, the phallic
blossom is *his* glory.

'My prince, snake, sun
fills me.'

Our mother is fierce, our mother
who fights at her lover's side.

She is the doe of Colhuacan
dressed in gentle plumage.

The sun goes to war
now the sun is going to war

men will be born and die
forever.

The doe of Colhuacan
dressed in gentle plumage.

Eagle, feathers, naked
unmasked, sun rises up
shines on her, naked
unmasked

the doe of Colhuacan
dressed in gentle plumage.

53 Song on the Feast of Atamalcualoyan

My heart sprouts flowers in the middle of the night.
Our mother is here, the goddess Tlazolteotl has come.

The spirit of corn was born in Tamoachan, the first place
on earth, in the realm of flowers, the first flower.

The spirit of corn was born where rain and mist rule,
where the children of man are made.

Day is going to shine, dawn will raise itself.
All the jewelled birds are sipping dew
in the realm of flowers.

On earth you stood up
in the middle of the square,
oh, Quetzalcoatl, prince.
There is happiness
beside the tree which blooms
different jewelled birds:
they become joyful.
Listen to our god speak,
listen to the jewelled birds speak!

There is no need to arm against our death.
There is no need to shoot arrows.
I must bring my flowers: the flower red as our flesh,
the white flower full of scent, from that place
where every flower blooms.

54 Song to Xippe Totec

You drunken cock, god, you drink the still night.
It's the blood you need to live.

Why do you deny it?

Let yourself burn,
put on your shining clothes!

Rise, shine,
god, you're sun streaming through mist
a rainbow, jade rain glistening on your back,
you're water coursing down the aqueduct, filling

you're the cypress shimmering like feathers
you're light green snaking shoots of plants

as it rains.

'You have done what I asked,
the hunger is gone,
so as to please me, so I can live.

I am the shoot of corn.
My heart is as fragile and precious as jewels
but it waits for the rainburst,
the gold shining through the rain.

My life dawns
on the horizon, once more
the man who is first in war
who comes out first to do battle
is born.
He grows strong.

Why should the light which flickers
in newly opened spirit of corn
go out?

I am the tender corn.
Your god is coming to you
from your mountains, over the ridge.

My life
is dawning
on me,

he grows stronger
he is born, once more

who is sun shining through rain
who is strongest
who is bravest in fighting surrounded by his enemies.'

55 Song to the Snake-Girl, Chicomecoatl

So many kernels on an ear of corn! Get up!
Wake up! You're our mother.
Don't leave us! We'll be orphans:

don't die, don't disappear to Tlalocan.

So many kernels on an ear of corn!
Wake up! You're our mother.
Don't leave us! We'll be orphans:

don't die, don't disappear to Tlalocan.

56 Song of Macuilxochitl

Here I am
straight from

where the flowers are moist with dew.
I'm dawn lighting up the sky

like a soft wind stirring
as you,

the land, the mother
also are lady of dawn

as the stars in the sky
also know
what will come, they too

wind which will nourish,
the light of dawn slowly
growing

in answer to
tassling corn . . .

[the rest of the poem is lost]

57 Cure for a Love Spell

Come!
here to me

woman in white
with your hair of smoke
your hair of mist,
your lush jade skirt,
mother, your rustling

Come !
here to me.

Watch me,

dark love
white love
blue love,

I've arrived, I am
the priest who owns the charms.

Mother, you,
whose skirt is stars:

did you do it?
did you put it in him?
earth

blue heart of rain, white heart of rain,
we're one as we writhe
together.

You did it!
You put it into him!

He's
at your feet.

3

Myths and Legends

58   Cloud-Serpent

Lady of the white jade skirt,
when your four-hundred offspring,
the cloud-snakes, northern stars,
were born, they fled and hid
in caverns of the earth.
Then you bore again,
this time five offspring, named
Eagle-Serpent
Cloud-Serpent
Wolf-Woman
Mountain-Hawk
Lord of the Canal.
They entered the water at birth,
stayed four days in the water
to fill out, and grow strong.
When they emerged, our Lady of the Earth,
you fed them from your breast.

The Sun gave his arrow
to the four-hundred cloud-snakes,
commanded them:
    'Take the shield and arrows.
    Find me drink and tribute!'
The arrow! It was precious,
made from sheaves of green quetzal feathers,
white plumes of the heron,
the zacuan's sunflower feathers,
pink from the redbreast, red from the troopial,
blue-green from the turquoise bird.
The Sun said:
    'Also remember your duty
    to the Lady of the Earth.'
But the four-hundred cloud-snakes
forgot their duty,

wandered hurling arrows at the birds,
gave their hearts and hands to pleasure. . . .
If they killed a tiger, they did not give it
to the Sun, though they dressed up in robes
to celebrate the deed. Their one pastime
was to dress themselves in plumage of the birds
and lie beside their women.
Their wrong was even greater than this:
for they drank the cactus wine,
wandered always half-crazed, overwhelmed with wine.

The Sun frowned. He called
the five offspring of Our Lady.
He gave to them an arrow made of thistles, thorns,
a shield like that the noble princes wear.
He said,
   'My children, . . .
   you must kill the four-hundred cloud-snakes.
   They have failed to call upon
   Our Lady and Our Lord.'
The five went to their duty, hid in an acacia tree
in ambush. The cloud-snakes,
seeing them within the tree, asked one another,
who was hiding there? Battle broke out then.
Eagle-Serpent slid into the body of the tree.
Cloud-Serpent dissolved into earth's body.
Mountain-Hawk became the mountain.
Lord of the Canal perched on the water.
Wolf-Woman, their sister, went to Tlachtli,
took her stand in the sacred court of the ball game.
The cloud-snakes circled the acacia tree:
the enemy was nowhere.
With their bodies the four-hundred
wove a hunting net, cracked the tree-trunk
with pressure from their bodies.
Eagle-Serpent leapt free
from the splinters of acacia:

the earth was set trembling.
Cloud-Serpent leapt from the entrails of earth.
The mountain burst with the din of landslide, fell,
and Mountain-Hawk leapt free.
The waters churned and boiled
and Lord of the Canal leapt from them.
Together, these four vanquished the four-hundred,
sacrificed them to the Sun, that he might drink
    their blood.
A few of the four-hundred survived,
came begging to the victors:
    'We have made you angry.
    But march now to Seven Caves,
    for they are now your caves.
    Enter your new palaces of earth!'
'Are they really ours? Are they to be our home?'
'You have won them in fair battle. They are yours.'
'Then we shall sit in peace within the mouths
of our own caves, our Seven Caves.'

One day two hinds came down from the mountain,
each hind with two heads. Behind them,
Precious-Turquoise and Arrow-Fish,
two survivors of the four-hundred, stalked.
They had wandered hunting on the rocky land
hoping to snare the two-headed hinds.
A whole night, then a day they trailed them,
until both hinds and men were weary. One hunter
    said,
    'Let us make two huts, one here, one there.'
When the huts were built, they said,
    'Still the hinds do not come.'
But they came suddenly — those who had been hinds
were hinds no longer. They had become two women,
beautiful, who cried out,
    'Precious-Turquoise, Arrow-Fish, where are you?
    Come to us! Come eat and drink!'

The hunters called them. Precious-Turquoise shouted,
    'Come, sister, come here!'
One woman came to him, saying,
    'Drink, Precious-Turquoise!'
He drank the blood she offered,
then lay beside her, pressed her body
with his body, bit her lips, at last
entered her. He said to Arrow-Fish,
    'I have eaten what is mine.'

The second woman called to Arrow-Fish
    'Come, my lord, come eat!'
But he did not call to her. He made a fire,
and as it flared he cast his body in.
The woman followed, threw her body on him.
The divine cactus bowl came down from heaven
and the woman threw her body into it. . . .
One of the Upholders of the Sky
saw the bowl was falling,
immediately hurled darts at the woman.
She leapt free, fled,
ran plaiting her hair, painting her body
as she ran, weeping that her lord
had been consumed by fire.

The gods, who made the years, heard of this,
hurried after her, to catch the woman
who was Obsidian-Butterfly. Arrow-Fish
ran before her. The gods caught up with her,
began to burn her body as she screamed.
From herself she hurled like sparks
numberless bright flints.
First the blue flint burst and flowered by her.
No-one took it up.
Next the white flint burst and flowered.
Cloud-Serpent caught it up, bundled it away.
Then the red, the yellow, the purple flints

sprung from her body, burst and flowered.
No-one took them up.
But Cloud-Serpent had the white flint
in a bundle for his god, packed it on his back.
He went off to his victories.

Cloud-Serpent went to capture the town of
      Huiznahuac.
On the road he met the woman Chimalman.
She came before him without robe or shawl,
naked, in her body. Cloud-Serpent did not look.
He fixed his shield, took four darts in hand,
cast them at the Chimalman.
The first flew above her;
the second struck her flank; it was deflected.
The third she caught up in her hand.
The fourth skipped past her,
fell among the agaves.
Cloud-Serpent threw four darts
and fled along the road.
The woman fled too
to hide in a place called Red Cave.

Cloud-Serpent came again to find her, in his fine robes,
to hurl darts. He went to her town, Huiznahuac,
saying to the women of Huiznahuac they should find
      her. . . .
In Red Cave they discovered her, said to her
  'On your account, Chimalman, Cloud-Serpent
    violates your sisters.'
They forced her to Huiznahuac. Cloud-Serpent
once again beheld her, naked as she stood,
but now her body painted red and yellow.
He prepared his darts. He overcame her with them, . . .
he lay with her at last.
Cloud-Serpent left her with his child.

Fiercely the child struggled
four days in her womb. When he was born,
she died. The child was male,
named One-Cane. Quilaztli, Lady Serpent,
brought him up at her hearth,
and when he was old enough for war
she took him to contend against his father.
He learned to fight in the Place of Turquoise.
There too he learned to hunt, and there
his four-hundred uncles, the cloud-snakes lived.
They had come to kill his father,
whose body they had buried in the sand.

One-Cane searched everywhere for his father.
The vulture heard him asking, said,
   'Your father has been murdered.
   He is buried in the ground.'
One-Cane dug up the body, laid it in a temple,
the temple of Cloud-Serpent on the hill
of Cloud-Serpent. . . .
Three of his cloud-snake uncles came to One-Cane.
They had murdered his father. They criticized him:
   'Why have you made a temple for your father?
   We will turn the hare, snake, tiger, eagle, wolf
   against you, they will punish you for this.'
The son replied,
   'What I do is right,
   What I do is right.'
He hastened all the same to call the tiger, wolf, and
     eagle.
When they came, he said,
   'Uncles, it has been decided, you cloud-snakes,
   I am to consecrate a temple with your blood.
   But you will not die, my animals.
   It is for you to kill and devour those
   who gave me cause to build this temple,
   killed my father. Devour them — it would be vain

to bring the victims roped together, back to back.'
Then he called the weasel to him.
    'Friend, we will dig and tunnel out
    chambers in this temple I have made.'
The weasel made a passage through which One-Cane
climbed up to the summit of Cloud-Serpent's temple.
His uncles, the cloud-snakes, cried out,
    'Let us fire the beams above his head!'
When eagle, wolf and tiger saw them come
they roared, and One-Cane unexpectedly lit
the sacrificial fire. His uncles prepared to fight.
The first cloud-snake slid up the steep temple,
but fell back again. One-Cane rushed on him,
split his skull with a stone. The other uncles,
furious, summoned the wild beasts with their flutes.
But the wild beasts came to kill them,
smother them with smoke of the burnt chili,
sting them, stretch their bodies out for torture.
They finally sliced their chests wide open,
squeezing out their hearts.

One-Cane Quetzalcoatl went to the land of the dead.
He came before the King and Queen of the dead.
    'I have come for the precious bones
    you have in keeping.'
The King of the dead replied,
    'Quetzalcoatl, what do you want them for?'
He said,
    'The gods are sad, and say among themselves
    they do not know who will inhabit earth.'
The King of the dead made conditions.
    'You will have the bones, but first
    you must sound my conch-shell
    and travel four times round my disc of jade.'
The conch-shell had no mouthpiece to be sounded.
Quetzalcoatl summoned worms to mine it,
the night-bee and the bumble-bee to enter it

and sound it with their drone.
The King of the dead heard. He said,
    'Well done. Take the bones of man.'
But he whispered aside to his servants,
    'Go tell the dwellers here that he has come
    to carry off the bones of man.'
Quetzalcoatl overheard, said angrily,
    'It is decreed that I must take the bones.'
To his companion, Lady Quetzalcoatl, he whispered,
    'Tell the dwellers here that I must take the bones.'
And he shouted aloud to them all,
    'I must take the bones of man!'
He lifted up the bones, half of man, half of woman,
bundled them on his back, carried them away.

Again the King of the dead whispered to his servants,
    'It is true, true, he has come to carry off
    the precious bones. Run, dig a trench before him,
    he will fall!'
They did this.
Quetzalcoatl, startled by a burst of quail-flight,
tripped and fell into the trench they made.
He lay as if dead, the bones scattered about him.
The quail began to peck and riddle them.
Quetzalcoatl came back to his senses, wept,
spoke to his companion,
    'Friend, how can this be?'
She replied in tears,
    'How can this be? How can this be?'
Quetzalcoatl gathered up the broken bones,
piece by piece, made a bundle of them,
and carried them upon his back to Tamoanchan,
the Place of Making.

When he came to Tamoanchan,
his companion, his Lady Serpent
Quilaztli Cihuacoatl, washed the splintered bones

in a precious glazed bowl.
Over them Quetzalcoatl bled his penis.
All the gods came then, five more beside Quetzalcoatl . . .
and bled themselves. For this reason we say,
   'Man was born of the gods',
because for us the gods shed their own blood.

The gods asked one another,
   'What will men eat?'
They began to search for corn. . .
Then the ant went to eat scattered grains of corn
on the Hill of Our Sustenance.
When Quetzalcoatl came upon the ant, he asked,
   'Where have you found corn to eat? Tell me.'
She would not reply, though he entreated her.
At last he touched her heart, she showed him
because Quetzalcoatl became a black ant,
conspired with another of that kind.
They forced the red ant to show them to the grain.
Quetzalcoatl took the grain to Tamoanchan
where the gods ate it, setting this word
on our half-formed lips,
   'We grow strong with corn.'

They asked,
   'What shall we do with the Hill of Our Sustenance?'
Quetzalcoatl strained to lift it on his back,
tying it with ropes, but failed. Then it was
that Oxomoco cast the grains like dice,
gambling with Cipactonal. . . When they had cast,
the rain-gods heaped great clouds above the earth:
blue gods like the bare sky, white, red and yellow gods.
The syphilitic god struck the hill, and rain-gods
caught the grains of corn, corn of many colours,
white, turquoise, purple, yellow; and other food:
beans, wild amaranths, lime-leaved sage and
    argemone.

They gather from the air whatever feeds us.

Now Quetzalcoatl contended with the gods of rain
in the Ball Court. They asked him to set the stakes.
   'My precious stones, my feathers.'
They said,
   'We will risk our precious stones, our feathers.'
Quetzalcoatl won the game. The rain-gods
changed their stakes. Instead of precious stones
they gave the tender ear of corn;
instead of quetzal feathers they gave green leaves
of the seeding corn. Angrily, Quetzalcoatl complained,
   'Is this what I have won?
   These are not gems or plumes!
   Take them away.'
The rain-gods said to him,
   'As you please.
   Give him jewels and rich feathers.
   We will take away our precious stones
   which are the grains of corn;
   our plumes, which are green leaves.'
They went off saying,
   'We will hide our gems and feathers.
   Four years of famine will possess the earth.'

59   Quetzalcoatl Flees

Then Quetzalcoatl was sad.
He thought back over how he had to go,
to leave his city, Tula. He thought of it
once more, and was determined.

They say he buried all: his shining gold,
smooth coral, and all else,
everything which was the richness of the Toltecs,
the artists. The precious things,
those we marvelled at, were all buried.
He put them all beneath the earth,
in underbrush,
in watercourses, deep in canyons,
inside the mountains.

The trees of fragile yellow cacao flowers and fruit,
the birds we treasured, in their plumes of solar fire,
left. He sent them on ahead of him
to the edge of the ocean.
And they went there.

Then he began his journey. And he came to a certain place
with a tree beside it, a fat full tree which springs
     up high.
He stopped beside it and saw himself.
He saw himself in the mirror and said,
     'I am old already',
and called the place
the Place Next To The Tree Of The Old Ones.
And he threw stones at the tree, a mosaic of stones;
the stones encase the tree,
then stay there as bark which covers the living tree.

It is how he saw himself in the tree,
root growing, lifting up into the crown.
As he went on his way, they were playing flutes.

Later, he came to a certain place
and sat down on the stone, leaned back on his hands:
as though the stone were clay,
the print of his hands stayed on it.
In the same way, the print of his buttocks on the stone
where he sat remained, gilded the stone.
It is how he saw himself: as the print of empty
    space on stone
which they called, 'Where There Is The Mark
    Of Someone's Hands.'

And he turned back towards Tula and cried.
His body shook with sobs like a cloud
as he cried. His grief became
twin plumes of hail, tears down his face,
cutting the rock as they landed, fell,
piercing the stone.

60 Quetzalcoatl Changes Form

And it is said that
he reached the edge of the sea in the year
        One-Cane.
He reached the beach of the great ocean.

He stood up
and began to cry.
He began to dress himself,
to put on the sacred clothing:
his green plumes of quetzal,
his sacred mask.

And then he stood up straight
and caught fire, set himself on fire,
and the flames embraced him.

And we know that when he burned
and his ashes flowed upward into the sky
all the birds whose feathers shine
came to see him, to watch —
all the birds who fly through air,

macaw with red plumes, indigo plumes,
the thrush with dappled feathers,
shining white bird, and the blue,
green, and yellow parrots —
all the most beautiful birds.

And when the ashes burned no more
his heart was at the zenith
and he was then called
'The Ruler of the Dawn.'

And we know besides:
he was not seen for four days, as he had gone
to the realm of the dead — he returned
with arrows in his fist, and after eight days
he became a great star.

And they say
it was only then
his reign began.

61   The Fall of the Toltecs

That shaman, owl man,
dressed himself in shining yellow feathers
once he had won. Then he planned that the people
should come together and dance.

So the crier went to the hill
and announced the dance, called out
to all the people. Everyone heard
and departed hastily to Texcalapa,
that place in the rocky country.

They all came, both nobles and the people,
young men and young women,
so many they could not be counted,
there were so many.

Then he began his song.
He beats his drum
again and again.
They join him in the dance,
they leap into the air,
they join hands and weave themselves
together, whirling round,
happily, happily.

The chant wavers up and breaks into the air,
returns as echo from the distant hills
and sustains itself.

He sang it, he thought of it himself,
and they replied.
As he planned, they took it from his lips.
It began at dusk and went on half way to midnight.
And when their common dance reached its climax,

numbers of them hurled themselves from cliffs
into gullies. They died, became stones.
They fell in the rapids and became stones.

The Toltecs never understood what happened there;
they were drunk with dancing, blind,
and afterwards they gathered there to dance
many times. Each time there were more dead,
more had fallen from the heights
into the rubble,
and the Toltecs destroyed themselves.

62   Tezcatlipoca's Song

I myself am the enemy.
I search out the servants and messengers
of my relatives
who are dressed in dark plumes,
who are plumes of rain.

I have to see them here,
not tomorrow or the next day.

I have my magic mirror with me
smoking with stars,
and my allies

until those others, my relatives, those
dark plumes of rain in glistening sun

until they're put away.

4

Songs of War

63

Heart, have no fright.
There on the battlefield
I cannot wait to die
by the blade of sharp obsidian.
Our hearts want nothing but a war death.

You who are in the struggle:
I am anxious for a death
from sharp obsidian.
Our hearts want nothing but a war death.

64

He
reliant on
the word
of the White Jackal
of Cohuacan. . .

seeking
flowers which make
drunkenness,
reliant on
our lord
the sun. . .

I too
it is said. . .

65

In spring the songs are not
of peace
the flowers not
of peace.

Everywhere is hatred.

66   Ometeotl to the Warriors

Where men rule
we rule,

it is the first law —

Sun, the mirror
which makes things shine and live
must war with night.

'They're going, they are ready!
Be drunk, be drunk,
warriors!'

It is our work,
it is the work
of the androgyne (who gave men life)

men do when they die
at dawn —

sun, the shining mirror to them,
making all things live.

67

Now we are convinced
the priest Cuauhtemoc . . .

. . .

Your heart spins around
noble Cuauhtemoc,
it is war, the eagle,
the earth convulses in his claws,
the sky spins around.
It's that he's been abandoned:
the barbarian's Deer-Man.

68

Flowers from the marl,
blossoms of plumage
made men's hearts
straight.
But the eagle's war flower
bent the hearts of men.
    And war princes passed
    away.
    Kings became bright
    hummingbirds.

. . .

No one perceives
the shield-flowers wither.
    We must go elsewhere, nowhere,
    move aside, make room for others.
    Earth is a loan to us.

. . .

A lily of wind,
the spinning shield —
dust like smoke rises.
The warriors' whistle
sounds in Tenochtitlan!

69

While the chiefs pass their time
in games

don't be last.
Your fortune is war.

The sun rises up at dawn
like an eagle.

He knows where
his life is.

70

Sunflower, flower of shields
spins around, rich, sweet-smelling
flower. It's in our hands
here, by the shimmering water,
in a plain flowing like water with men,
the god will pick them, flowers.

71

Sacred crazy flowers,
flowers of bonfires,
our only ornament,
war flowers.

72

How do they fall? How do they fall?
These hearts, ripe fruit for harvest.

Look at them,

these fall, the hearts —   oh our arrows
these fall, the hearts —   oh our arrows

73 Poem of Warriors

None so strong, none so prized
as the eagle in flight,
the tiger whose heart is a mountain:
   they submit to serve.
The yellow tiger weeps.
The white eagle forms a war cry
through his hands.
These are the princes. . .

There was the shaping of eagles,
making of tigers — the princes.
   There was a plain of battle
where the tigers learned their colour,
where the eagles swayed.
   A place
where Ipalnemoani
takes whom he will. . .

Princes,
eagles and tigers, into each others' arms
while the shields sound, they come together
to the festival.
There will be captives. *y yao ay yaha*

They are scattered, they fall on us,
the flowers of war which are used
to please the giver of life, the sun.

Where it is boiling, where everything is upturned,
in the place of war,
where there is glory to have,
place where the rattles sound,
where a cloud of dust opens up. *ohuaya ohuaya*

The flowered war need never end; it stays
by the river: there
the tigers as flowers,
the flowers of shields, have opened their petals,
there, in the place where rattles sound.
     ohuaya ohuaya

There is the sweet garden of tigers: they will fall
in the midst of the plain.
They will pour their fragrance upon us,
on us who wish glory and fame. *ohuaya*

The ungrateful flowers, those flowers of hearts
have sprung up on the battlefield, at the edge of the
     fight

where the princes find honour and glory. *ohuaya*

The shields of eagles mesh with the standards of
    tigers.
Shields with green quetzal feathers are given out.
The helmets, with gold-coloured plumes, moving
    like a snake,
shaking there in the boil, and the Chalca and
    Amaquemecan warriors
leap into battle, they who came, together, in great
    confusion. *ohuaya*

With a sharp noise
the arrow broke,
its obsidian point splinters,
upon us,
the dust spreads,
is boiling. *ohuaya ohuaya*

75

Where are you going? Where are you going?
To war, to the sacred water.
There our mother, Flying Obsidian,
dyes men, on the battlefield.
The dust rises
on the pool of flame,
the heart of the god of sun is wounded.
Oh Mactlacueye, oh Macuil Malinalli!
War is like a flower.
You are going to hold it in your hands.

76

Rattles shake the plain
where Tlacahuepantzin was left behind:
with yellow flowers
he is going to sweeten the realm of death.

You are only hiding in the north,
in Seven Caves,
where acacia grows, where the jaguar howls,
where the eagle roars, where everything is made.

You are the quechol, flame-coloured,
where you fly over the plain,
through the realm of death.

77   Homage to Tlacahuepan

With shields, you paint nobility.
With arrows, you write battle.
Now, you dress yourself in plumes
and paint your face with chalk for the sacrifice.
Oh Tlacahuepan,
you are going to take them with you into the realm
    of mystery.

Oh Tlacahuepan, you are over the princes.
You cry out, the eagle who is red answers you.
Like a dancer, who is to die,
with whistling hands,
and at the end, to the realm of mystery.

Your song is like a mottled jaguar.
Your flower is like the spread wings of an eagle.
Oh my prince, as a dancer, who is to die,
there in the clash of shields.
How beautifully you play your drum.

You garland the nobles with flowers of the eagle,
the gathering of friends, oh dancer, who is to die,
the wine of precious flowers makes men drunk and
    brave
and he will dress himself with his flowers and songs
in the realm of mystery.

Perhaps the Mexicans are singing there too.

78   Elegy for Tlacahuepantzin

God of rattlesnakes!
your flowers tremble —
tiger, eagle warriors roar.

The War Prince befriends
and favours us. But flowers
of flesh wither.
There, by the drums,
they are shuddering like women.

The war-dead! in the flowering water
with shields and banners raised!
Not by spears or arrows
the precious flower falls.
   The flower made of human body
will never taint the moss
of Moctezuma, will not ever
sprout again in Mexico.

Smoke-stained, your red bird of light:
you pass, prince Tlacahuepan.
Smoke-stained, the god renews him.
God, god tears your flesh away!

. . .

. . . desolate my heart,
I see a child
tremble like a feather
shattered.

I go to the garden
where princes
make each other proud with flowers.
I see a child. . .

79   Nezahualpilli's Lament

Drunk,
my heart is drunk:
dawn
and the zacuan bird is singing
over the shield stockade,
stockade of spears.

Tlacahuepan, neighbour, friend,
rejoice! You with your shaven head
are like one of the Cuexteca tribe —
drunk with the flower waters,
by the shore of bird-river,
with your shaven head.

Rocks fracture
jewels, precious feathers,
my princes:
those who were drunk with death
in the plain of water,
on the shore — there,
the Mexicans among cactus.

The eagle screams,
warrior with the tiger's face roars,
O prince Macuil Malinalli;
there in the field of smoke,
field of red. . .
it is right, it is right
the Mexicans make war!

. . .

My prince
blood-stained, death-yellow
the lord of the Cuextecas,
his skirt now black as the zapote fruit.
The glory of war clothes my friend
Tlacahuepan — in the mystery
where one perhaps lives on.

My prince
Matlaccuiatzin is drunk
with the flower of war, death-yellow
lord of the Cuextecas,
bathed in the liquid of war.
Together they go
where one perhaps lives on.

Sound the tiger's trumpet!
Eagle on the war-stone screams,
there on the carcasses of our dead lords.
The old men pass, Cuextecas
drunk with the flower of shields.
In Atlixco they dance!

Sound the turquoise drum.
Cactuses are drunk with fallen flowers;
you with the heron head-dress,
you with the painted body.
They hear him, go beside him,
birds with flower-bright beaks
accompany the strong youth
with the tiger shield. He has returned to them.

I weep
from my heart, I, Nezahualpilli.
I search for my comrades
but the old lord is gone,
that petal-green quetzal,

and gone
the young warrior.

Let the sky-blue be your dwelling!
Are Tlatohuetzin and Acapipiyol coming
to taste the water here
as I am weeping?

(*Nezahualpilli*)

80

I see the eagle and the tiger warrior.
Their glory saddens me who will depart
from earth, from the friendship of warriors.

Ipalnemoani,
you fly to us, bird
with a sword in your claw
and darts. Perched
in your own temple you preen
and sway among the drums.

Rain of down:
like a sacred heron you preen
and sway among the drums.

You tint the fire
and colour the throne of warriors.
My friends, you are princes
in the springtime palace.
What does Ipalnemoani require of us?

You will not remain long
in this palace. Nezahualpilli,
our friend, deserts you. War
sends up its flowers. Some grow,
some wither. They are eagles, tigers of war.

Those that wither
come back to you,
Ipalnemoani.

A march of warriors
to the region of Death:
every lord descended
but returned
in a flash
to live in the face of the sun.

Now they wander
the endless plain of the dead.

81

They look with envy,
they look with anger
at Huexotzinco.

It is surrounded with thistle swords.
It is blockaded with arrows,
the city of Huexotzinco.

Metal gongs and drums of tortoise shell
roar in Huexotzinco.

But Tecayehuatzin and Quecehuatl rule there,
and flute and song ring out in Huexotzinco.

82

With upturned shields
we died in Chapultepec,
we died among the rocks.

The princes were borne off
in all four directions:
they are weeping at their fate.

King Huitzilihuitl,
a banner flutters in his hand
there in Colhuacan.

83 Songs of the Fallen

i (Prose Account of the Conquest)

This is how the Mexican, the Tlaltelolca perished. He
abandoned his city. There in Amaxac we all waited.
And we had no more shields, we had no more weapons,
we had nothing to eat, and so ate nothing. And all
night long the rain was falling on us.

ii

As was their duty
they went slowly to the ruler and the judge
and were levied.

They sang only songs at Acachinanco,
to take heart
when they came face to face with the fires in Coyoacan.

iii

We mourned for ourselves, our lot.
Broken spears lie in the by-ways,
we have torn out our hair by the roots.

Palaces stand roofless, blood-red walls.
Maggots swarm the squares and huts.
Our city walls are stained with shattered brains.

Water flows red, as if someone had dyed it,
and if we drink
it tastes of sulphur.

In grief we beat our fists

against the walls of our mud houses,
a net of holes our only heritage.

Our strength was in our shields
but shields could not resist this desolation.

We have eaten cakes baked of linnets,
chewed dog-grass that tastes of nitre;
we have swallowed lumps of clay, lizards, rats,
farm soil turned dry dust, even maggots. . .

iv

The lament extends like a cloud
and on the market town tears fall.
Already the Mexicans have fled across the lake.
They are like women. Everyone flees.

'Where are we going?'

'Oh, friends!'
and later,

'Has it happened?'

They have abandoned the capital already.
Smoke rises, the mist
is spreading.

Weep, my friends,
and know that by these deeds
we have forever lost our heritage.

Appendix

Poems from Contemporary Oral Tradition

Four Otomí poems

Yesterday it flowered.
Today it withers.

. . .

I am going says the cow.
I am going says the ox.
They are going down the mountain says the wasp.
I will follow them says the firefly.

. . .

The river goes by, goes by
and never stops.
The wind goes by, goes by
and never stops.

Life goes by
and never comes back.

. . .

Sun shines on a dewdrop:
it dries.
In my eyes, in mine, you shine:
I, I live.

Three Quechua poems

Farewell

Today I'm supposed to leave.
I won't go.
I'll go off tomorrow.
When I leave you'll see me
playing a flute of flies' bones
with a spiderweb as my flag,
an ant's egg for my drum
and my hat
will be the nest of a hummingbird.

I Raise a Fly

I raise a fly
with gold wings.
I raise a fly
with glowing eyes.

It brings death
in its eyes of fire.
It brings death
in its gold hair
and its lovely wings.

I raise it
in a beerbottle:
no one knows
if it drinks,
no one knows
if it eats.

It roams at night
like a star.
It wounds and kills
with its light of blood,
with its eyes of fire.

It steals love
for its eyes of fire.
It hides the blood
in the night,
the love, in its heart.

Insect, every night,
fly of death
in a green bottle —

I raise it,
loving it so much.

But no one knows
this is so;
this is so
if I let it drink,
if I let it eat.

What Harm has she Dreamt

Her long hair is her pillow
the girl is sleeping on her hair.
She cries blood
she does not cry tears
she cries blood.
What is she dreaming?
what harm is she dreaming?
Who hurt her?
who hurt her heart like this?
Whistle to her, whistle, whistle
little bird
so she wakes
so she wakes now
whistle whistle
little bird.

Six Lacondon poems

Fishing for the Name of a God

I do this, I move my hand for him, whose name is in the sky, for him, whose name is in my hand. Don't let a false name in my hand. Take me, receive me, give me your name, do not let a false name in my hand. For him whose name is in heaven, in the house of stars, I say his name in the sky. Don't let my hand lie. Tell your name in the house of stars. Take my spirit in, into the house of stars. Take me. In this trunk, the root of . . . [the god] . . . For him, I say his word with my hand. Don't let my hand disappear. He tells the truth. He is finishing his word here in my hand. He will come up if it's well said. He finishes his word in my hand.

Purification of Grains of Copal Incense

Break! Split open! I burn you. Live! Wake up!
Don't sleep! Work! I wake you to life.
It's me who brings you up to life in the censer.
It's me who makes you fresh. It's me who builds your
    bones.
It's me who makes your head. It's me who builds
    your lungs.
I'm the one who builds you, your maker.
This sacred drink is for you.
This offering of *balch'e* is for you.
It's me who brings you to life. Wake! Live!

. . .

Every time I lift my foot,
every time I lift my hand,
when I move my tail,
I hear your voice from far away.
I'm almost asleep:
I look for a fallen tree,
I'm going to sleep in the fallen tree.
My skin, my foot, my head,
my ears, are striped.

. . .

I'm setting the virgin table
for you, god.
I offer you thirteen gourds, cool and virgin words.

Beans Offered to the Fire in the Name of the God

Here are the first beans.
I give them to you, god.
I will eat them.

**Balch'e Offered to the Brazier in the
    Name of the Gods**

Take it yourself and enjoy it, take it with pleasure.
It is far away, the flavour of vanilla has gone away.
Take it and enjoy it, life goes over into you, breath
goes over into you. Take it happily, the smell of
vanilla is far away, the smell is gone.

Eight Huichol Shaman poems

I'm the tree of air
and I can change myself
to a man or a woman.
As a man
I take women.
As a woman,
I take men.
I am the most stoned
madman,
the craziest in the world.
And that is why
I'm called
Taweakme.

Antonio Bautista, who did not hear the voice of Tamatz, the blue deer god

I went there. Where
the hills can be seen.
I heard nothing. There
where the hills
can be seen.
I heard nothing. There
was nothing I heard.

. . .

The flowered road
goes here.
It goes to Viricota.
They said you
were around here
and I came to look for you.
Though I'm not like you,
though I've sinned,
I'm around here
and I've come for you.

. . .

Who knows why
the hills stood up
there in Viricota?
Who knows why
the hills speak
there in Viricota?

. . .

Viricota, Viricota
who knows why
the roses cry?
Who can say?
Who can foresee?
Who knows why
the roses cry?

Tutuyyuave Viricota Nieme

. . . The blue flower, the beautiful flowers
of Viricota have become
the feathered wands of Tataveri.
They are sacred flowers.
They are the songs of peyote.
They are memories of Viricota
sung by the gods of Viricota.

A crinkled flower calls to us.
Whose crinkled eyes are seeing us?
They are the eyes of the peyote
which was born in the ground of Viricota
and so they always watch us.
When the clouds meet each other
the flower becomes a rainbow
in fresh leaves of many colours.
We see this all,
yes we see it.
But we do not know
what it means to tell us
when the flower becomes
rain and light wind.
They must be very sacred things,
very hidden. We can only know
these songs, here in Viricota.
Flower, crinkled flower, rukurita,
you are a tray of flowers,
you are the flower of peyote
and at the same time, Teinietzika
our goddess, flower of corn.

First Peyote Song

There were the waves, coming out from the waves,
the sea, and after the sea came the gods, all of them.
The gods passed by like flowers, in the form of
flowers, coming after the sea and they came to the
placenta where it springs from the flesh of the womb
which bore them. And from the placenta the cloud,
from the cloud the heavenly temple, from the temple
the deer who was then corn who became cloud
once again and rained on the cornfield.

The ocean spoke to the gods of the five directions
and the Blue Buck came out of the sea with Mari
the fawn and other tiny deer.

Then, on the altar, the arrow and deer head were
seen, there on the mat of herbs. The gods
understood what the arrow said. It turned to cloud.
And the message of the arrowhead which had
turned to rain

& they went to the field and left their offering there.
What's happening in the cornfield? What's
happening in our mother's womb, in Tatei
Urianaka?

We have to know what happens there, what happens
here.

They hid in the mountains and attended the
heavenly birth. From the centre, the mat, from the
altar, were born cane and tender tassles and ears of
corn, round gourds, and the yellow whirlpool flower
of *tuki* which they picked and rubbed in the palms
of their huge hands,

with the dust yellow as pollen, they painted sunrays
on their faces. They said, 'The herbs on the altar
were the Deer's cradle and now it will be his funeral
shroud since they'll lay him there when they kill
him in the mountains.'

When they said this, the Blue Deer Marrayueve
        stood up on the altar
and off in the north in the south in the east in the west
blue deer appeared.

Second Peyote Song

The flowers are flying, they spin around, once around
Burnt Hill where the Deer and the altar were born
from the heart of our fathers' father, fire.

The gods are talking, they do talk to us and no one
can say what they mean.

But here is the arrow. You see it stuck in the centre
in the centre of the sacred mat of herbs. It understands
the language of the gods. There next to it is the snake,
blue Jaikayuave who translates the gods, who knows
the arrow's language.

The rain is born from the altar of herbs, the rain
is set loose and you hear what the gods say:

'Brothers, it's time to make the arrow of rain. The cord
comes out of the mouth of rain, the plumes of rain,
the feathers of arrows, the clouds pile up
and the gods of the four directions take shape.'

They talk among themselves. They understand each
        other.
They agree. They all agree:

Viricota, Aurramanaka, Tatei Nakaw, Tatei Urianaka,
Saint Andrew.

They all leap up in the air and spin around the place
where all was born, and fall to earth where they see
the feathered arrow which marks the place where the
deer was born.

There
is his feathery funeral cradle, the sacred altar.
And our brother Tamatz Kallaumari

is stretched out on it,
resting.

Glossary

This brief glossary attempts to define some of the more important allusions to people, places, plants and animals in the poems. It is not complete, but no major allusion is left unglossed.

ACACHINANCO   A city slightly south of Tenochtitlan (q.v.) in the Lake of Texcoco. It was connected by a causeway both to Tenochtitlan and Coyoacan (q.v.).

ACAPIPIYOL (ACAPIOLTZIN)   Tutor to Nezahualpilli (q.v.); an adviser to Nezahualcoyotl (q.v.).

AMAQUEMECA (AMECAMECA)   City near the foot of Popocatepetl, the volcano, near the border with the Tlaxcaltecans, traditional enemies of the Aztecs.

AMAXAC   A city in the Valley of Mexico, where many of the Aztecs fled when Tenochtitlan, their capital, fell to the Spanish.

ANAHUAC   Mexico-Tenochtitlan, the name means 'surrounded by water' in Nahuatl. It is used to refer both to the capital city and to the area of the empire.

ARGEMONE   A kind of poppy with a delicate white flower and characteristically thorny leaves, used in some Aztec medicines.

ATAMALCUALOYAN   A feast celebrated once every eight years. It derives its name from the ritual eating of 'water tamales', the unseasoned maize-cakes steamed in skins of the maize ear. The feast is probably associated with planting, and seems to have taken place at the conjunction of Venus and the Sun.

ATLIXCO   A city in the Valley of Puebla, over the mountains from the Valley of Mexico, where the Aztecs suffered a severe defeat at the hands of the Tlaxcaltecans.

AYOCUAN   King of Tepexic, also known as Ayocuan Xochimecatecutli. In the poem, Ayocuan is presumably a warrior, 'he who shot his arrow into the sky.' Another Ayocuan, King of Tecamachalco, is the poet referred to in the Dialogue of Poets which took place in Huexotzinco (q.v.) Three of the poems in *Cantares Mexicanos*, some of the finest, are attributed to the latter Ayocuan.

AYOPECHTLI Aspect of Chalchiuhtlicue, goddess 'living in the turtle's nest' at the edge between land and water, thus presiding over the transition from watery womb to daylight.

BALL COURT The sky; the ball game enacts the mythical struggle of Huitzilopochtli and Tezcatlipoca, the sun and the 'smoky shield' of the night sky.

CACAMATL Son of Nezahualpilli, last king of Texcoco.

CACAMATZIN Cacamatl Cuauhtli, poet, noble of the city of Chalco.

CHALCA (adj.) Those of Chalco, a city on the south-eastern shore of Lake Texcoco.

CHAPULTEPEC A hill of rock originally on the shore of Lake Texcoco close to the island city of Tenochtitlan, and strategic to the Aztecs for defence. Moctezuma's fresh-springs still flow there. The name means 'hill of the grasshopper'.

CHICOMECOATL seems to be the aspect of Chalchiucihuatl, 'lady of jade', earth goddess of fertility, which is that of sterility. She was portrayed as a pubescent girl.

CHIMALMAN Mother of Ce Acatl Topiltzin Quetzalcoatl (q. v.), of the town of Tepotztlan. She figures in the poem 'Cloud-Serpent'. The father of her child was Mixcoatl ('cloud-serpent').

COHUACAN (COLHUACAN, CULHUACAN) City south of Mexico-Tenochtitlan, one of the cities of the Valley of Mexico founded after the collapse of the Toltec empire in the late twelfth century, prior to the arrival of the Aztecs.

COYOACAN One of the older cities in the Valley of Mexico, on the southern edge of Lake Texcoco.

CUAUCUAUTZIN (CUACUAUTZIN) Poet-prince, son of Tezo-zomoc, ruler of Azcapotzalco, near Tenochtitlan.

CUAUHTEMOC Last Aztec king. He led the Aztec nation in active resistance after Moctezuma (q.v.) had been stoned to death while attempting to convince the people to submit to the Spaniards. He succeeded Tlacaelel, who died of small-pox. Cuauhtemoc's surrender to Cortez (1521) marked the end of the Conquest. He was later tortured and killed on Cortez's orders during the march to Honduras. His name means 'falling eagle.' Poem 67 refers to a priest of the same name.

CUECHTLAN Huastecan (q.v.) city. The word implies 'place of shells'.

CUEXTECA Members of the tribe which lived in the land of the Huastecs, on the Gulf Coast. They wore their heads shaven.

DEER-MAN Tlacamazatl, the priest, a magical warrior in the spirit-world.

DIALOGUE OF POETS Tecayehuatzin (q.v.) brought together a number of poets at Huexotzinco, his city, for a dialogue (*Cantares Mexicanos* f. 9-12). This meeting provoked perhaps the finest flowering of poetry of friendship and Life, and many of the poems we have translated are from this happy occasion.

HUASTECS The Huastecs were a tribe noted for their original handicrafts, but more important culturally, they were a source for many of the subversive fertility rituals and beliefs which were anathema to the Aztec establishment.

HUEXOTZINCO A major city in the Valley of Puebla, from which much of the remaining poetry came. The Huexotzincans were hostile to the Aztecs. (See also Tecayehuatzin).

HUICHOL One of the most isolated tribes in Mexico, who speak a Nahuatlan language and live in the mountains of the Sierra Madre Occidental in the present Mexican states of Nayarit and Jalisco. They retain a culture largely unaffected by outside sources and are famous for their beautiful embroidery. Their mythology is rich and complex, concentrating on the relations between men, gods, deer, peyote, corn and water-goddesses of springs, rivers and lakes. It is very probably derived from archaic sources prior to the Aztec sun-cult. The Huichols have been studied in depth by Fernando Benitez who devotes the entire second volume of his *Los Indios de México* to them. There is also much information on them in Karl Lumholtz's *Explorations in Unknown Mexico*.

HUITZILIHUITL The second Aztec king, ruling 1395-1417.

HUITZILOPOCHTLI The god of sun and war (see Tezcatlipoca).

ILILIN (ILILLIN) A flower.

IPALNEMOANI 'He for whom we live'. Also known as 'Tloque Nahuaque', the 'god of the immediate vicinity'. Ipalnemoani is a central philosophical concept in Nahuatl literature. As a mythical personality he represents the unity of all aspects of the universe. He is particularly significant to the 'Toltec' school of poets (see Introduction), among them Nezahualcoyotl (q.v.) and his son. At the time of the Conquest, these 'reactionary' poets were attempting to return to the purer, classical Toltec tradition which antedated the Aztec supremacy in the Valley of Mexico. It was typified by a persistent sense of ephemerality, a reaction against the war-cult, and a seeking after permanence in friendship and beauty.

LACONDON   A small group of Maya living along the Usumacinta River in southern Mexico.

MACUILXOCHITL   Lord of flowers, games, poetry.

MACUIL MALINALLI   A friend of Nezahualpilli (q.v.), who lamented him in his moving elegy after the Aztec defeat at Atlixco. His name, derived from the date sign, probably of his birth, means 'five-grass-tuft'.

MATLACCUIATZIN (MATLALCIHUATZIN)   Mother of Nezahualcoyotl (?).

MEXICANS   i.e., Aztecs, called individually 'Mexica'.

MIMICH   See Xiuhnel.

MIMIXCOA   Cloud-serpents, identified with the Milky Way.

MOCTEZUMA (MOTECUZOMA, MONTEZUMA)   Moctezuma Xocoyotzin was the second Aztec emperor of that name (the first was Moctezuma Ilhuicamina). A cultured and religious man, he was taken prisoner by Cortez' plotting, while the Spaniards were his guests. He was stoned to death by a mob in an attack on the Spaniards' stronghold. He ruled from 1509 to July, 1520.

MONENCUAUHTZIN   Poet from the city of Huexotzinco (q.v.) where the great 'Dialogue of Poets' took place in the palace of Tecayehuatzin (q.v.).

MOTENEHUATZIN   Lord of Teupil, one of the poets at the 'Dialogue of Poets' at Huexotzinco.

MOQUIHUIX (MOQUIHUIXTLI)   Lord of Tlaltelolco, a city near Tenochtitlan, occupying a sister island to the great capital. His wife, the sister of the king of Tenochtitlan (Axayacatl) had such foul breath that her husband turned to his concubines for pleasure. His wife complained, his mighty brother-in-law grew angry, attacked Tlaltelolco, and annexed it officially to the Aztec city [León-Portilla].

NEZAHUALCOYOTL   1402-1472, King of Texcoco. He is the most famous of the Nahuatl-language poets, considered by his contemporaries to be the best master of the classical style. Many tales are told of his wisdom as judge, public servant, philosopher, and teacher.

NEZAHUALPITZINTLI (NEZAHUALPILLI) 1464-1515, King of Texcoco, son of Nezahualcoyotl, and almost his equal in fame as a poet. He was not so just a man as his father, suffering from foibles like those mentioned in the note to 'Cuacuautzin's Sad Song' (poem 46). Four poems in the *Cantares Mexicanos* are ascribed to him. His name means 'prince who fasts'.

NINE PLAINS Metaphorical term for the steppes of Northern Mexico which the Aztecs passed through in their migration south.

NONOHUALCO (NONOALCO) City of inhabitants of the Valley of Mexico before the Aztecs' arrival; it was incorporated into the metropolis of Mexico-Tenochtitlan.

OMETEOTL-OMECIHUATL Lord and Lady of duality; represented graphically in the Codices as an androgynous god at the centre of the universe, the navel, as the source of all other manifestations of deity. Perhaps to be identified with Huehueteotl, god of fire, since fire had a dual and creative aspect as movement, *ollin*, life in the interaction between heaven and earth. See also under Quetzalcoatl.

OPOCHTLI A god associated with Tlaloc, visualized as ruling over lake and marsh; inventor of net, spearthrower snares and oars. Probably birdlike himself, a tutelary spirit.

OTOMÍ The major non-Nahuatl linguistic group in Mexico. These poems were collected by Garibay in the town of Huizquilucan in the mountains just outside Mexico City. The Otomís are probably the tribes referred to classically as Chichimecas.

PLACE OF ORIGIN Seven Caves or Tamoanchan (q.v.).

QUECHOL Bird with reddish or rose-coloured plumage.

QUECHUA The predominant Andean indian culture, descendants of the classical Inca. Today they occupy much of the highlands of Peru, Bolivia and Ecuador. Further translations of contemporary Quechua poetry are in John Brandi's *Chimborazo*.

QUETZAL Bird with long blue-green tail plumes, more highly valued among the Aztecs than gold. The bird, native to Central America, is now the national symbol of Guatemala.

QUETZALCOATL   The most famous of the Mexican gods, his name is usually interpreted to mean 'plumed serpent'; he is identified with the god of wind (Ehecatl) and with Venus. As a legendary prince, he was famous for his wisdom and asceticism, until tempted by his adversary, Tezcatlipoca (q.v.), his stellar opponent. Many of the poems translated, especially the long narratives, recall his parentage and his development both as God and as King of the Toltecs. If there was a tendency towards monotheism in pre-Columbian Mexico, it centred on him — his name has recently been interpreted as 'plumed twin', the god of duality, 'Ometeotl'. His nature is complex, and in him many divergent powers focus.

QUILAZTLI   'She who makes green things grow', the aspect of the Earth Mother concerned especially with the sprouting of plants. In her sexual aspect as a fertility goddess she is represented as an eagle with a mask encircled with blood; she is bloody, as woman giving birth were often called 'warriors'. As Quilaztli Cihuacoatl she is earth-snake-woman, feathered in the leaves of young plants.

SEVEN CAVES   Chicomotzoc, the Place of Origin (q.v.) of the tribes. See also Tamoanchan.

TAMOANCHAN   Also known as Tlalocan, a mythical place, 'the house from which we descend', the place of creation. The souls of the dead live there as spirits. It is the region of mystery and at once the paradise of vegetation. Associated with Tlaloc, the rain god, it is swathed in mist, a place of fecundity. In it, the tree of life grows, and sometimes Ipalnemoani (q.v.) is said to live there.

TECAYEHUATZIN   King of Huexotzinco, a poet, and host of the 'Dialogue of Poets', several fragments of which (*Cantares Mexicanos* f. 9-12) are translated in this book. Miguel León-Portilla argues in his excellent edition and translation of the text that Huexotzinco was the centre of a cultural renaissance which, at the time of the Conquest, had begun a cultural revolution against Aztec domination.

TEMILOTZIN   Aztec prince-warrior and poet, a hero during the Conquest when he fought beside Cuauhtemoc. As a poet, his duty was to encourage friendship through his song. Captured by Cortez' Indian vassals, he jumped into the sea. The Chronicles record: 'Temilotzin would not listen, would not be held back. They saw him throw himself into the water. He swims off towards the sun. Malintzin calls after him, saying, "Where are you going? Come back! Come back!" He did not listen, he went away, disappeared. No one knows if he reached the other shore of the sea, if a serpent devoured him, a lizard ate him, or if a big fish finished him off . . . but this way he took his own life. No one killed him.'

TENOCHTITLAN   Capital of the Aztec empire, site of the present-day city of Mexico, the city 'surrounded by water' described by Bernal Diaz as a place of golden palaces equal in wonder to the romance of Amadis of Gaul. The city was set in the midst of Lake Texcoco, connected by causeways to the mainland.

TETEOINAN   The goddess of the earth. In this form her name means 'mother of the gods'. As Tonantzin, she is 'our mother', the mother of mankind. In another aspect as Tlazolteotl, she is 'devourer of filth', since she fed on corpses, symbolized as hearts. As Coatlicue, 'the lady with the skirt of snakes', she represented the fertile earth.

TEXCALAPA   'The stony place'.

TEXCOCO   A major city on Lake Texcoco which held ascendancy before the Aztec arrival. It is the source of much of the remaining verse left to us. It was also the site of the last Aztec religious rising against Spain, and one of the first schools set up by the early friars was located there.

TEZCATLIPOCA   The god of sorcerers, eternally young. He is also known as 'the enemy' (cf. poem 62) and as a patron of warriors is associated with Huitzilopochtli, the sun and war god. Originally he symbolized the night sky, thus his name: 'the mirror that smokes'. One of the codices tells how he, jealous of wise Quetzalcoatl (q.v.), lured the good king into drunkenness and incest with his sisters. Then he showed him his face in the 'mirror that smokes', and Quetzalcoatl, penitent for his guilt, migrated south and set to sea on a raft of rattle-snakes, or (in variant legends) built himself a pyre, burned his body, and left the world with the promise that he would return in the year 'One-Cane'. When that year came, Cortez arrived.

TLACAHUEPANTZIN (TLACAHUEPAN)   A ritual figure, a young man sacrificed at the feast of Toxcatl as one of the 'cloud-snakes' (cf. 'Cloud-Serpent', poem 58) who returns to the Seven Caves, place of Aztec origin. In 'Nezahualpilli's Lament' (poem 79) he was the king's warrior friend, killed in battle.

TLALOCAN   Place of Tlaloc, god of rain, an earthly paradise of flowers hidden in mountains. Cf. Tamoanchan.

TLALTECATZIN   A lord of Cuauhchinanco, a major Aztec poet, present at the 'Dialogue of Poets' at Huexotzinco.

TLALTECUHTLI   Earth goddess. Garibay cites the myth in which Quetzalcoatl and Tezcatlipoca brought her down from the sky and she fought so hard that her body was torn apart. To console her the gods ordered that 'they made trees and flowers and herbs from her hair, tiny flowers and grass from her skin, springs and small caves from her eyes, rivers and caverns from her mouth, and valleys and mountains from her nose.'

TLALTELOLCA   Adj., the inhabitants of Tlaltelolco, a northern subdivision of the city of Tenochtitlan (q.v.).

TLAXCALA   City-state north of Tenochtitlan; the major opponent to Aztec hegemony in the north. Cortez found his best Indian allies here. The city was culturally rich and a centre of humane worship on the Toltec (q.v.) model. The first Indian converts to Catholicism were made here.

TLAZOLTEOTL   See Teteoinan.

TOLTEC   A Nahuatl-speaking tribe. Their capital was Tollan, and four centuries before the Aztecs arrived their empire extended throughout central Mexico. Their great achievements in art and architecture, poetry and astronomy, were widely dispersed, and later tribes looked back on them as a classical culture whose ideals were to be emulated, though the Aztec establishment frowned on their cult of Quetzalcoatl, their tendency towards humane monotheism. As an historical figure, Ce Acatl Topiltzin Quetzalcoatl was the ruler of the Toltecs, but it is hard to segregate the historical from the legendary figure in the lists of his exploits. He is said to have turned a nomadic tribe of barbarian warrior-plunderers into artisans, poets and philosophers in one generation.

TOTOQUIHUATZIN   King of Tlacopan (1431-1469). His name has the sense of 'rain of birds'.

TULA   The Toltec (q.v.) capital, Tollan.

TZINITZCAN   A brightly-coloured small bird, sometimes said to be the hummingbird.

VIRICOTA   Mythical place of origin for the Huichols, where all transactions between gods and man took place, and Tamatz Kallaumari, pre-eminent deer god, comes to earth. The present-day peyote-gathering pilgrimage takes the pilgrims to an actual Viricota in the western part of San Luis Potosi.

XIPPE TOTEC (XIPE) A Huastec god of fertility. He is represented as a priest wearing the flayed skin of his victim. In this form he represents the rebirth of vegetation in spring, and is associated with rain and moistness. He also represents sexual fertility, and as such is worshipped in the form of a phallus. As 'he who drinks night', seems also to be identified with the sun.

XIUHNEL AND MIMICH Two of the survivors of the four hundred cloud-snakes, they are represented as hunters, each with two deer heads on his shoulders. Their names mean 'precious turquoise' and 'arrow fish' (cf. 'Cloud-Serpent', poem 41).

XOCHIPILLI See Xochiquetzal.

XOCHIQUETZAL Goddess of flowers and love, she is associated with rain and vegetation. Her husband is a young warrior, the sun, whose love she receives, conceives his children, innocent of the fact that they will be warriors. She is associated with Xochipilli, who is more particularly a sort of Muse figure, presiding over 'flower and song' and dancing; and with Macuilxochitl, 'five flowers'. Her own name means 'plumed flower'.

XOLOTL One of the more ancient gods, the god of twins, identified as the twin brother of Venus. Mythically, he is a sorcerer, master of transformation and metamorphosis.

YOYONTZIN Nezahualcoyotl.

ZACUAN Bird with yellow or gold plumage.

ZAPOTE A black fruit of the hard-wood zapote tree.

Sources

The main editions used in making the translations were:

BENITEZ, FERNANDO   *Los Indios de México*, Mexico, 1968
DURAN, FRAY DIEGO   *Historia de las Indias de Nueva España . . .*, (two volumes), Mexico, 1867, 1880
GARIBAY, ANGEL MARIA K.   *Llave del Náhuatl*, Mexico, 1940
   Epica Náhuatl, Mexico, 1945
   Historia general de las cosas de la Nueva España, Mexico, 1956 [his edition of the Florentine Codex]
   Historia de la Literatura Náhuatl (two volumes), Mexico, 1953
   Veinte himnos sacros de los Nahuas, Mexico, 1958
   Poesía Náhuatl (three volumes), Mexico, 1964 [his edition of the *Cantares Mexicanos* and *Romances de los señores de la Nueva España*, with a translation which forms the basis of most of the versions in this book]
LEÓN-PORTILLA, MIGUEL   *La filosofía Náhuatl, estudiada en sus fuentes*, Mexico, 1956
   Los antiguos mexicanos, através de sus crónicas y cantares, Mexico, 1961
POMAR, JUAN BAUTISTA   *Relación de Tezcoco*, Mexico, 1891
SODI PALLARES, DEMETRIO   *La Literatura de los Maya*, Mexico, 1968

In these references, CM indicates *Cantares Mexicanos*, RS *Romances de los señores de la Nueva España* and VH *Veinte himnos sacros de los Nahuas*. The translator is indicated by his initials; where none appear, the translation is a joint version.

1 RS f.17, *MS*	7 CM f.19, *MS*
2 RS f.20, *MS*	8 RS f.35, *MS*
3 CM f.17, *MS*	9 RS f.7, *MS*
4 CM f.21, *MS*	10 RS f.16, *MS*
5 CM f.25, *MS*	11 CM f.22, *MS*
6 CM f.15, *EK*	12 CM f.67

13 CM f.35, *MS*
14 CM f.17, *MS*
15 CM f.14
16 RS f.16v, *EK*
17 CM f.71, *EK*
18 RS f.38, *EK*
19 VH 19 *ll.* 15-22, *EK*
20 CM f.12, *EK*
21 CM f.30, *MS*
22 CM f.19, *MS*
23 RS f.2, *MS*
24 CM f.2, *EK*
25 CM f.22, *EK*
26 CM f.9, *EK*
27 CM f.35
28 CM f.9, *EK*
29 CM f.12, *EK*
30 CM f.71, *EK*
31 CM f.9-12
32 CM f.13r, *EK*
33 CM f.69, *EK*
34 CM f.69, *EK*
35 CM f.9
36 CM f.22
37 CM f.17, *EK*
38 CM f.11, *MS*
39 RS f.14, *MS*
40 CM f.9-12, *EK*
41 RS f.5, *MS*
42 CM f.35, *MS*
43 CM f.17
44 CM f.10, *EK*
45 CM f.9-12, *EK*
46 RS f.26-7, *MS*
47 VH 4, *EK*
48 VH 5, *EK*
49 VH 7, *EK*
50 VH 9, *EK*
51 VH 12, *EK*

52 VH 13, *EK*
53 VH 14 i and ii, *EK*
54 VH 15, *EK*
55 VH 16, *EK*
56 VH 20, *EK*
57 VH appendix V no. 3, *EK*
58 Sahagún's Anales de Cuauhtitlan in *Epica Náhuatl*, *MS*
59 *Llave del Náhuatl* text 7, *EK*
60 Ms de Cuauhtitlan f.7, *EK*
61 *Llave del Náhuatl* text 5, *EK*
62 VH appendix V no. 1, *EK*
63 CM f.9, *EK*
64 RS f.9, *MS*
65 CM f.11, *MS*
66 VH appendix I no. 1, *EK*
67 RS f.14, *EK*
68 CM f.20, *MS*
69 RS f.42, *EK*
70 RS f.8v, *EK*
71 RS f.8v, *EK*
72 VH appendix I no. 3, *EK*
73 CM f.20
74 CM f.18, *EK*
75 CM f.70
76 CM f.22
77 CM f.23, *EK*
78 RS f.31, *MS*
79 CM f.55-6, *MS*
80 CM f.2, *MS*
81 CM f.32, *EK*
82 CM f.12, *EK*
83 *Cantos de los Vencidos* (Mexico, 1968), *MS*, *EK* (ii)

Appendix

All translations by *EK*.

Otomí poems: from *Historia de la Literatura Náhuatl*, vol. 1.

Quechua poems: from Raquel Jodorowsky's Spanish in *El Corno Emplumado* 12.

Lacondon poems: from Demetrio Sodi, op. cit.

Huichol poems: from Benitez, op. cit., pp. 136-7 and 550-1.

Further Reading

The books listed (all in English, or English translation) are easily accessible to readers, either in libraries or from bookshops. They are only a few of the large number of important studies in the field. Those marked with an asterisk are possibly the most interesting and cogent.

BERNAL, IGNACIO *Mexico Before Cortez, New York, 1963

BRINTON, DANIEL Ancient Nahuatl Poetry, Philadelphia, 1887

CASO Y ANDRADE, ALFONSO * The Aztecs: People of the Sun, Oklahoma, 1958

CLAVIGERO, F. S. The History of Mexico (tr. Charles Cullen, two vols.), London, 1787

DIAZ DEL CASTILLO, BERNAL * The Conquest of New Spain (translated by J. M. Cohen, Penguin Books, 1963)

DURAN, FRAY DIEGO The Aztecs: The History of the Indies of New Spain (tr. Doris Heyden and Fernando Horcasitas), Oklahoma U.P.

LEÓN-PORTILLA, MIGUEL *Aztec Thought and Culture, Oklahoma, 1963

*Pre-Columbian Literatures of Mexico, Oklahoma, 1968

NICHOLSON, IRENE Firefly in the Night, London, 1959

The X in Mexico, London, 1965

Mexican and Central American Mythology, London, 1967

O'GORMAN, HELEN Plantas y flores de Mexico, Mexico, 1963

SÉJOURNÉ, LAURETTE Burning Water: Thought and Religion in Ancient Mexico, London, 1957

SOUSTELLE, JACQUES Cosmology of Ancient Mexico, London, 1957

Daily Life of the Aztecs, Penguin Books, 1961

SPENCE, LEWIS The Gods of Mexico, London, 1923

SPINDEN, HERBERT Ancient Civilizations of Mexico, New York, 1933

THOMPSON, J. ERIC Mexico Before Cortez, London, 1933

VAILLANT, G. C. Aztecs of Mexico, Penguin Books, 1952

Edward Kissam is a poet and documentary video producer. After studying for a doctorate in Comparative Literature, he taught at San Francisco State University and Sonoma State University. His collections of poetry include *The Sham Flyers* (1972) and *Jerusalem and the People* (1974). Among his video productions are four pieces on farmworkers in the 1980s: *Voices From the Edge of a Dream, 49 Years in the Land of Plenty, La Vida Loca*, and *Choices Down the Road*. Mr. Kissam grew up in Mexico and first began publishing poetry there.

Michael Schmidt was born in Mexico in 1947. He studied at Harvard and Oxford and is now special lecturer in poetry at the University of Manchester (UK). He is editorial director of Carcanet Press and General Editor of the bimonthly literary magazine *Poetry Nation Review*. Mr. Schmidt has published several collections of poetry, two critical monographs on British poetry, and he has edited anthologies and critical surveys. His first novel, *Green Island*, has been published in the United States by Vanguard Press.